Edwin Wilbur Rice

Our Sixty-Six Sacred Books

How They Came to Us and what They Are

Edwin Wilbur Rice

Our Sixty-Six Sacred Books
How They Came to Us and what They Are

ISBN/EAN: 9783337779962

Printed in Europe, USA, Canada, Australia, Japan

Cover: Foto ©Lupo / pixelio.de

More available books at **www.hansebooks.com**

OUR

Sixty-Six Sacred Books:

HOW THEY CAME TO US, AND WHAT THEY ARE.

A POPULAR HAND-BOOK FOR COLLEGES, SUNDAY-SCHOOLS,
NORMAL CLASSES AND STUDENTS, ON THE ORIGIN, AU-
THORSHIP, PRESERVATION, CHARACTER AND DIVINE
AUTHORITY OF THE CHRISTIAN SCRIPTURES.

SECOND EDITION WITH ANALYSIS AND QUESTIONS.

By EDWIN W. RICE, D. D.,
*Author of People's Commentaries on Matthew, Mark, Luke,
and John, etc.*

PHILADELPHIA:
THE AMERICAN SUNDAY-SCHOOL UNION,
1122 CHESTNUT STREET.
NEW YORK: 8 & 10 BIBLE HOUSE.

NOTE TO SECOND EDITION.

IN this Edition some inaccuracies have been corrected, information on MSS. brought up to date, and some facts on the circulation of the Bible have been added. The Analysis and Questions, prepared by Anna D. Lewis, of Carleton College, and an Index by James G. Rice, are features which will greatly facilitate the use of the Manual. The call for a second edition so soon, and the translation of a chapter (V) into German, and its re-translation into English for the American press, give gratifying evidence of deep interest in studies about the Bible and wide appreciation of this Manual. EDWIN W. RICE.

PHILADELPHIA, March, 1892.

INTRODUCTORY NOTE TO FIRST EDITION.

THE members of a Bible Study Circle, composed of advanced students and teachers, requested the author to give a series of lessons or studies upon the origin, authorship, preservation, character and divine authority of the books of the Bible. These lectures were afterward written out and issued in *The Sunday-School World*. The kindly reception given to the studies, and the call for them by a wider circle of Bible students, has led the author to revise, enlarge and adapt them to more general use. His hope is that they may lead to a more intelligent knowledge of our sacred books, and a more reverent faith in the Christian Scriptures.

EDWIN W. RICE.

PHILADELPHIA, October, 1891.

CHAPTER I.

INTRODUCTION. 1. The three foremost nations of the world in: (1) literature and learning; (2) science and discovery; (3) commerce and wealth, are Christian. They are Great Britain, Germany and the United States of America.

2. Ask these three great nations for their greatest book in respect of: (1) its circulation and popularity; (2) its influence on their national life; (3) its deep hold on the heart of the people, and they will unhesitatingly and unitedly answer, The Bible.[1]

3. The educated Mongolian or Malayan is eager to know about this great book. The inquiring Asiatic mind bristles with questions. What kind of a book is that Bible? What is it about? How did you get it? Who wrote it? How long ago was it written? For whom was it made? Has everyone in Christian lands a copy? Is it found in other languages? In how many? How was it written? How preserved? Who translated it into your Christian tongues? Why is it not found in all languages? Even among Christians, thoughtful and wise, these and a hundred

---

[1] Bible comes from the Greek *Biblia*, plural of *Biblion*, " little book," a diminutive of *Biblos*, " book." The Latin plural also, *Biblia*, is used by Chaucer in Canterbury Tales, and by Wyckliffe in the Preface to his translation, and as a title by Coverdale.

other questions start up demanding intelligent answers. In fact, every Christian ought to have some knowledge of the history, the origin, contents, and purpose of the greatest book in Christendom. These questions are worthy of scholarly and clear answers. Let us address ourselves to them. We will trace the history of the book up the stream of time. Beginning with what is most familiar and best known we will proceed step by step to what is less known.

4. THE ANGLO-AMERICAN VERSION. The latest English translation of the Bible is the Anglo-American or Revised Version, printed at Oxford and Cambridge, England, 1881–1885. It is known as the Anglo-American or *Revised Version* to distinguish it from the *Common Version* frequently called also the *Authorized Version,* and the *King James Version.*[1]

5. A revision of the *Common Version* was suggested by Prof. Selwyn in 1856, but not then approved by scholars. It was again urged by Bishops Wilberforce, Ellicott, Ollivant, and others of England, in 1870, and a committee of 16 (8 from each house) was appointed by the Convocation of Canterbury, with authority to invite other eminent Biblical scholars to join them in the revision.[2] A committee of American scholars of all the leading Protestant bodies of America (as in Great Britain) was formed in 1871, to co-operate with the British committees in revis-

---

[1] It is called the *Common Version* because it is the English translation now most widely used by English-speaking people; the *Authorized Version* because it was supposed (but erroneously) to have been formally approved or authorized by royal authority, and *King James Version* because it was made during the reign of James I., King of England.

[2] The Convocation of York declined to join in the revision, but many of the greatest scholars of England, Scotland and America were engaged in the work.

ing the Common Version of the Bible of 1611. The whole number of scholars engaged upon the *Revised Version* was 101, of whom 67 were British, and 34 American.[1]

6. The revision of the New Testament was completed in 1881 and issued May 17 in England and May 20 in America. The Old Testament was finished and the entire revised Bible issued in May, 1885. The issue of the revised New Testament in 1881 awakened a profound interest among all English-speaking peoples. "It is the literary event of this century," says Schaff. Millions of copies were sold in a few months.[2] More than twenty reprints at once appeared in the United States. For once popular interest in the newspapers was supplanted by that in the revised Scriptures.[3] The revised New Testament was sought by crowds at the bookstores and news stands; it was hawked on the streets, and read on the cars, in the omnibus and in the stage coach. The entire text of the revised Testament was telegraphed to two daily newspapers in Chicago and printed complete in morning editions! When the revised Old Testament was completed four years later the entire revised Bible was issued, but its advent awakened comparatively little interest. Public curiosity and excitement exhausted itself apparently upon the New Testament.

7. *Why Revise the King James Version?*—(1) To remove obsolete words and phrases, as "let" in the sense of "hinder;" "ear" meaning "to plow;" "prevent" in

---

[1] The *active* members (in 1879) were 79, namely, British 52, American 27. See *Bible Revision*, Philadelphia, pp. 10-12.

[2] Oxford had orders for a million of copies before publication; Cambridge probably for as many more. Two million copies were sold. in London. Nearly half a million were sold in New York and Philadelphia, besides many American reprints published soon after its completion.

[3] See Schaff, *Companion to Greek Testament*, p. 403 ff.

the sense of "going before;" "carriages" meaning "baggage" or "luggage." (2) To give the meaning of the original with greater precision, to keep step with the progress of knowledge in the Greek and Hebrew of the original Scriptures. (3) To conform to a purer text now attained. More than 500 valuable MSS, a score of Ancient Versions, and writings of 100 Christian Fathers have been examined and collated, in order to perfect the original text of Scripture.

8. *Will the Revision be Generally Accepted ?*—Time alone can definitely answer. It is widely used with the Common Version in Sunday-school lesson helps; some prominent religious journals use it instead of the Common Version, and eminent Biblical scholars constantly refer to it in critical works. It has not, however, come into very general use among the people, nor among the churches.[1]

9. *Objections to the Revised Version.*—Three serious obstacles exist in the popular mind to its general introduction: (1) The omissions and changes in passages long familiar and of forms of expression deeply endeared to the Christian heart.[2] (2) Printing the text in paragraphs, disregarding the breaks of chapter and verse. Although the new arrangement is a gain in getting the sense of a passage, it hinders quick reference to a desired clause or verse.

---

[1] The Baptist Convention at Saratoga, N. Y., 1883, agreed to adopt and circulate the Anglo-American revision with the American changes put into the text, *along with* the Bible Union Version. Some churches among the Baptists and Congregationalists use the *Revised Version*, and it is occasionally read from the pulpit in a few churches of other denominations.

[2] One of the most serious omissions, to the common reader, is the doxology to the Lord's Prayer, Matt. 6 : 13. Among other changes are: "Every Scripture given by inspiration is profitable," etc., 2 Tim. 3 : 16; "Ye search the Scriptures," John 5 : 39, and numerous texts in the Psalms and Prophets.

Marking the chapters and verses in the margin does not overcome this objection; for the eye misses the familiar breaks in the text and does not readily catch the verse or clause desired. (3) The omission of chapter headings and running head-lines at the top of each page. To satisfy the ordinary reader, these must be inserted. He will not accept the excuse that their insertion *might* lead the translator into "the province of the commentator." The words added in the text (in italics) in the Revised and in previous Versions are often equivalent to a comment, and should be excluded by a strict application of that rule. The outlook for the new version to displace the old is not yet very promising. It has been sharply criticised by some able Biblical scholars in Great Britain and America.

10. It must be remembered, however, that the present "Authorized Version" was also criticised and was from thirty to fifty years in coming into popular and universal use; but it finally displaced the popular Genevan Version and the Bishops' Bible, which had been favored by royal and by ecclesiastical authority.

11. *American scholarship* was tardily, though on the whole fairly, recognized in the work. Over 900 American suggestions in the New Testament were adopted by the British revisers.[1]

---

[1] Among the more important American renderings which the English revisers were unwilling to adopt were: (1) "demon" or "demons" for "devil" or "devils" in such phrases as "to cast out devils." The Bible speaks of many evil spirits, but of only *one* devil; (2) "who" or "that" in place of "which" when applied to persons, and to substitute modern forms of speech for such archaic forms as "wot," "wist," "hale;" (3) "sheol" wherever it occurs in the Hebrew text for "grave," "the pit," and "hell," and omit these words from the margin; also put "Jehovah" where found in Hebrew, for the "LORD" and "God;" (4) a more accurate designation of coins; (5) omit the title "Saint" and "Apostle" in the headings to New Testament books. See "Ap-

12. *Conservative Plan.*—The principles guiding the re-visers were very conservative. They were to make "as few alterations as possible," as already stated. About 36,000 were made in the New Testament, but proportionately fewer in the Old Testament. They were to limit the "expression of such alterations to the language of the authorized or earlier versions." About 6,000 changes were made in the Greek text of the New Testament; but comparatively few changes in the Hebrew and Chaldaic text of the Old Testament.[1] The original text followed (Hebrew and Greek) was to "be that for which the evidence is decidedly preponderating." No radical changes could be made under the rules adopted, nor could an essentially new translation be introduced under cover of revision. Even those who criticise the infelicitous English it occasionally uses, admit that the renderings generally represent the original more accurately than previous English versions. If this proves to be true, the Revision can afford to wait; truth is stronger than prejudice and error, and will finally prevail. Let us now consider the translation upon which the Revised Version was based.

13. THE KING JAMES OR "AUTHORIZED VERSION." This version of the Bible was proposed by Dr. Reynolds,[2] of

---

pendix" to Revised Testament, and Companion to Revised Version by A. Roberts, Am. ed., pp. 177 ff. Also Companion by Schaff.

[1] Of the nearly 6,000 changes made in the Greek New Testament text, and over 36,000 changes in the English New Testament of the Authorized Version, the great majority are of trivial or minor importance, and would not be noticed by the common reader.

Of the 179,914 words in the Revised New Testament 154,526 are retained from the "Authorized Version." See R. Wendell, Revised New Testament.

[2] Dr. Reynolds was a Puritan and President of Corpus Christi College, Oxford. He was stoutly opposed by Bishop Bancroft, but James I. was vain, and aped Solomon for wisdom.

Oxford, and ordered by James I., in 1604. The king appointed fifty-four translators (probably suggested by the universities); but the work was delayed for three years, and the list we have gives only forty-seven scholars certainly known to have entered upon the work. They were divided into six companies. Each company was assigned a portion of the Bible (including the Apocrypha) to translate; two companies meeting at Westminster, two at Oxford and two at Cambridge.[1]

14. *Principle of the Version of 1611.*—This translation was to conform to the Hebrew and Greek texts; but the then current Bishops' Version "was to be as little altered as the truth of the original will admit." The older versions, as Tyndale's, Coverdale's, Whitchurch's and the Genevan, might also be used when they agreed "better with the text than the Bishops' Bible."

15. *King James' Version a Revision.*—In fact, therefore, the King James Version was a revision, rather than an entirely new translation. This is also implied by the title-page in our common Bibles. [2] When the scholars appointed by King James had completed their revision or translation, six of their number (some say twelve) met to review the work and correct the printer's proofs. It was issued in a black-letter folio volume by R. Barker, with a fulsome dedication to

---

[1] The first company at Westminster had the books of the Old Testament to 2 Kings; the second company had the Epistles of the New Testament. The first company at Oxford had the prophetical books from Isaiah to Malachi; the second had the four Gospels, Acts and Revelation. The first company at Cambridge had the other Old Testament books, and the second had the Old Testament Apochryphal books.

[2] "The Holy Bible, translated out of the original tongues; and with the former translations diligently compared and revised." Some English Bibles add, "By his majesty's special command." "Appointed to be read in churches."

the king and a pedantic preface written by Dr. Miles Smith, giving the reasons for the work and the principles guiding those who did it.

16. *Why called "Authorized Version."*—The King James Version is popularly, though not accurately, called the "Authorized Version." On the title-page as now printed in England is a notice, "Appointed to be read in churches." But this was not on the first edition of the New Testament of 1611, nor on several editions of the Bible issued in the first five years after the issue of the King James Version. The most diligent search of officials and scholars has failed to find any evidence that the version was ever publicly sanctioned in 1611 by convocation, privy council, parliament or by the king. It gained the title possibly because the work was *ordered* by the king. The version (for it was not a new translation) gradually displaced the existing versions (the Bishops' and the Genevan), and won its way to popular acceptance by its superior merits. But the contest was a long one. The King James Version was attacked for lack of fidelity to the Hebrew and Greek text. Romanists likewise accused it of misrepresenting Scripture to favor Protestantism. Arminians charged it with a Calvinistic bias, Puritans with a leaning to the Church of England, and others with favoring monarchical notions. (See 1 Pet. 2 : 13.)

17. For more than twenty years after the issue of the King James Version the Genevan Version was widely, if not generally, used in private and public worship. Though no edition of the Bishops' Bible was issued after 1608, the New Testament of the Bishops' Version appeared in at least five editions from 1608 to 1618. Editions of the Genevan Version of the New Testament and of the Bible continued

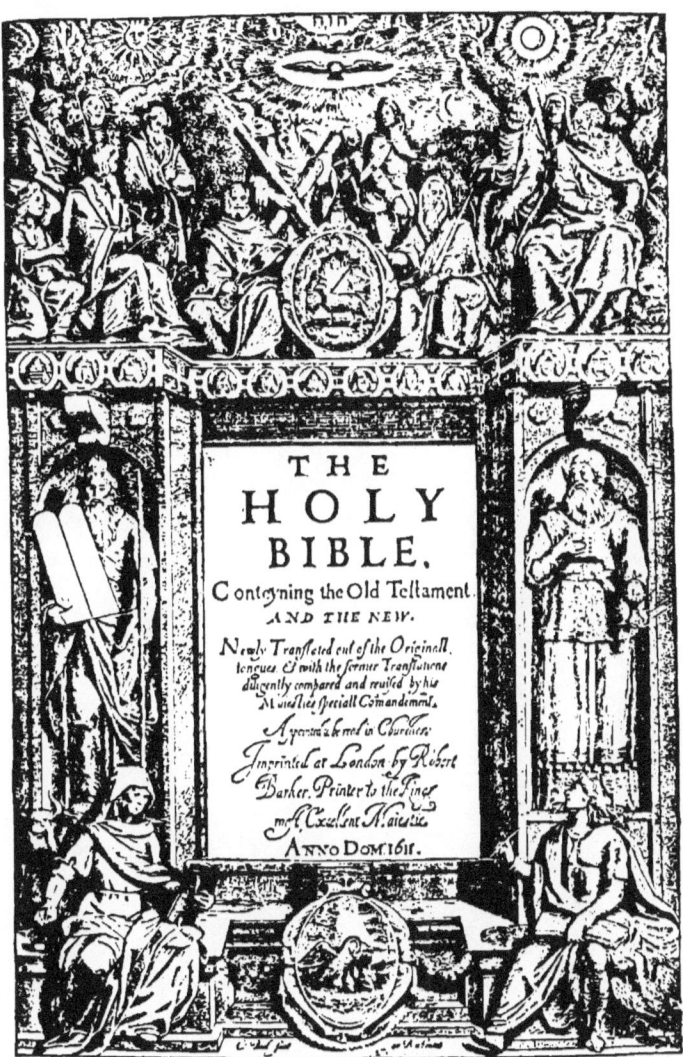

THE
HOLY
BIBLE,
Conteyning the Old Teſtament,
AND THE NEW.

Newly Tranſlated out of the Originall
tongues: & with the former Tranſlations
diligently compared and reuiſed, by his
Maieſties ſpeciall Comandement.

Appointed to be read in Churches.

Imprinted at London by Robert
Barker, Printer to the Kings
moſt Excellent Maieſtie.

ANNO DOM. 1611.

FACSIMILE OF KING JAMES VERSION, 1611

to be issued freely up to 1644. Texts for sermons were chosen from the Genevan or other versions than the so-called Authorized Version, even by bishops and those high in authority, for many years after 1611. Even as late as 1653 parliament considered a bill for the appointment of a committee to revise the King James Version. This project failed, as parliament soon after dissolved. The house of Stuarts was restored to the rule of England, and the version of 1611 was left to win its way over all previous versions and to remain the popular English version since that period.

18. *Changes in the Version of* 1611.—Comparing a common English Bible of now with a copy of the first issue of 1611, marked differences are at once seen. Not only is a difference seen in the forms of the letters and in the spelling of many words, but in the readings of numerous passages.[1] After the folio edition of 1611, the King James Version appeared in an octavo form in 1612, and in an edition omitting the apocryphal books in 1629. The errors of the earlier issues were corrected in editions of 1616, but especially of 1629 and 1638.[2] Bishop Lloyd's edition, of London 1701, was the first that gave chronological dates in the margin, based chiefly upon the chronology of Ussher.

---

[1] For instances of this, see Scrivener's Preface to the Cambridge Paragraph Bible. Even the folio edition of 1613 differs from that of 1611 in over four hundred places.

[2] The errors of some editions gave them celebrity, as the "Vinegar Bible" (a splendid and costly one), Oxford, 1717, so called from a misprint of *vinegar* for *vineyard* in heading of Luke 20. The "Wicked Bible" (8vo. 1631) was so called from the omission of "not" in the seventh commandment, and Laud fined the king's printers £300 for their carelessness in printing it. A copy of the "Wicked Bible" is in the Lenox Library, New York. There is a German Bible, 1731, with a similar blunder. The "Breeches Bible" was so called from the reading of a Genevan edition, "made themselves breeches," Gen. 3 : 7.

Additional marginal references were inserted by Dr. Paris in 1762, and by Dr. Blayney in 1769.

19. *No Standard Edition of the King James Version.*— The Committee on Versions (1851–56) of the American Bible Society found twenty-four thousand variations in six different editions of the Authorized Version, and recommended improvements, which were adopted, including revisions of the chapter headings.   So great was the popular opposition to these changes, that the society was compelled to discontinue issuing the amended edition and return to the old issues, with all their variations and imperfections. This, however, shows how strong a hold the Bible has upon the popular heart.   We have therefore no standard edition of the "Authorized Version" of the English Bible.   The King James Version of the English Bible belongs to the golden age of English literature, the age of Shakespeare and Milton and the greatest of English classics.   It possesses the strength of the Saxon, the grace of the Norman French, and the dignity of the Latin, harmoniously mingled into vigorous and perspicuous English.

CHAPTER II.

EARLY ENGLISH VERSIONS.

1. *The Common Version a Growth.*—Our common English Bible, the King James or so-called "Authorized Version," is the outgrowth of many preceding versions, and the fruit of more than two centuries of labor by many eminent Biblical scholars.

2. *The Douai Version.*—The great eagerness of the people for the Bible in their own tongue compelled the Romanists to issue a version, as they state, "specially for the discovery of the corruptions of divers late translations and for clearing the controversies in religion of these days."[1] The New Testament was published at Rheims, 1582. The Old Testament was translated about the same time, but was not published until 1609-10 at Douai or Douay, and the Douai Bible complete at Rouen, 1633-35. The work is believed to owe its origin to William Allen, one of the founders of the college at Douai. The translation is from the Latin Vulgate, and was made by Gregory Martin and three or four other English scholars. Modern editions of the Douai Version differ widely from the original version. Cardinal Wiseman says, " To call the Roman Catholic version now in use the version of Rheims and Douai is an abuse of terms. It has been altered and mod-

---

[1] From title-page, Rhemish New Testament, 1582.

ified till scarcely any verse remains as it was originally published."[1]   The Roman Church has never been friendly to vernacular translations of the Bible, and hence the Douai Version has had a comparatively small circulation.   Though it may have contributed some minor improvements to the King James Version, it is not in the line of succession of that version.   The next link immediately back of the King James Version is the Bishops' Bible.

3. THE BISHOPS' BIBLE was prepared by Matthew Parker, Archbishop of Canterbury, and ten or fifteen men of learning, most of whom were bishops; hence its title Bishops' Bible.   It was completed, and a copy presented to Queen Elizabeth, in 1568.   Parker issued a revised edition in 1572.   This version is also sometimes called *Parker's Bible*.

4. *Why Made.*—The Genevan Version (see p. 21) with brief explanatory notes had become the Bible of the common people, having displaced the Great Bible of Cranmer, used by the clergy and in the church services.   As the Great Bible was not as accurate a translation as the Genevan, and could not regain its former popularity, a new version was attempted which would be more acceptable to royalists than the Calvinistic and republican ideas reflected in some of the comments of the version by the Puritan reformers of Geneva.

5. The Bishops' Bible was completed in about three years.   The rules laid down by Parker were conservative and simple : (1) To follow the common English translation used in the churches, except where it varied from the original ; (2) to use chapter and verse divisions as in Pagninus and Munster ; (3) to make no " bitter notes;" (4) to change indelicate words to " more convenient terms."   It

---

[1] Wiseman's Essays, vol. i. pp. 73–75.

contained marginal notes, references and brief comments explanatory of the text.[1]

6. Several editions of the Bishops' Bible were issued; the last in 1608. In 1571 Convocation ordered that every archbishop and bishop should have a copy of this version, "of the largest volume," placed in his hall or dining-room for the use of servants or strangers, and also a copy in every cathedral, and if possible in every church. This was clearly at that time the so-called "Authorized Version." It supplanted the Great Bible, but the Genevan held its place with the people.

7. THE GENEVAN VERSION was made by English reformers who found a refuge in Geneva from the persecution of Queen Mary, and was published in 1560.

8. *Genevan New Testament, 1557.*—Three years earlier a translation of the New Testament into English was made at Geneva by William Whittingham (aided perhaps by others), who had married Calvin's sister.

9. *The Genevan Bible* was a distinct work, begun in 1558 and completed in 1560. The translation was the joint work of a company of learned men, among whom were Coverdale, Knox, Whittingham, Goodman and Cole. But the translation of the New Testament in the Genevan Bible was a careful revision of the Genevan New Testament of 1557.

10. *Popular Merits of the Genevan Bible.*—(1) The translation was from the best original texts then known. (2) Its form was a neat quarto instead of the clumsy folio.

---

[1] Some of the comments are curious: Rom. 11 : 8 reads, " the spirit of remorse;" the comment is, "pricking and unquietness of conscience." Isa. 66 : 3 reads, " he that killeth a sheep for me *knetcheth* a dog ; " the note explains, "that is, cutteth off a dog's neck;" a much-needed note !

(3) Explanatory notes on hard texts (Swiss in doctrine and politics) were given in the margin.   (4) The type was clear Roman in place of the unsightly black letter formerly used.   (5) The text was broken into chapters and verses after Stephens' Greek Testament (1551) and Pagninus' Latin (1528), but adding numerals at the beginning of each verse.   (6) Chapter headings, references and (in Henry's edition, 1578) a Bible dictionary of value.

11. A careful revision was made by L. Tomson, in 1576, and the Genevan was the first Bible printed in Scotland, 1579.   It was the first *complete English translation of the Bible direct from the Hebrew and Greek*.[1]   The comments were lucid, vigorous, sometimes dogmatic, but generally practical.   It quickly gained a wide popularity.   At the accession of the Roman Catholic Mary, the public use of the English Bible was forbidden in churches ; all copies that could be found were burnt (with an army of martyrs), and not a single Bible was printed in England during her five years' rule.   When Elizabeth became queen in 1558, the Bible was again freely read.   Not less than 130 editions of the Genevan Bible were printed, over 90 of them before 1611.   It retained its popularity for a generation after the King James Version appeared.[2]

12. *The Great Bible* (1539) was edited by Miles Coverdale under direction of Thomas Crumwell.   Paris was

---

[1] The Old Testament shows that Coverdale's Great Bible was carefully consulted, and the New Testament that Tyndale's Version was followed.   It is nicknamed the " Breeches Bible," from its rendering " made themselves breeches," Gen. 3 : 7.

[2] Yet the King James editions of 1612–13 had a title-page the facsimile of the Genevan (heart-shaped oval with twelve tribes and twelve apostles in margin), and other editions copied the form and style of the Bishops' Bible in order to supplant more easily these popular versions. Eadie, *Hist.*, vol. ii. p. 291.

FAC-SIMILE (REDUCED) OF TITLE PAGE OF THE GREAT BIBLE.

famous for the excellence of its paper and type. Coverdale went thither to have it printed. But the work was interrupted by order of the Inquisition and many sheets seized. Most of these were recovered, and, with types, presses and men, brought to England, where the work was issued in 1539. It has an elaborately engraved title-page designed by Hans Holbein, the most famous wood-engraver of his day.[1] From its large size, 14 x 9 inches, this work was called *The Great Bible.* A second edition in 1540 had a preface by Cranmer, from which it has been inaccurately called *Cranmer's Bible.* It is likewise called *Whitechurch's* or *Whitchurch's Bible,* after the name of the printer. The version is mainly a careful revision of *Coverdale's Bible* of 1535, and is of special interest because the Psalter and the Scripture selections in the communion service of the English Church Prayer-book are from the Great Bible. It remained the "Authorized Version" for twenty-eight years; indeed, strictly it is the only "Authorized Version," for neither the Bishops' nor the King James Version ever had *formal* royal approbation or authority.[2]

13. *Coverdale's Bible,* 1535, which the Great Bible closely resembled, was based largely upon the Latin Vulgate and German Versions, as the title to his New Testament honestly states.[3] The German versions used were doubtless Luther's and the Zurich; Pagninus and the Latin Vulgate, and Tyndale, probably make up the "five interpreters" Coverdale says he followed. The chief merit of

---

[1] A fac-simile of the title-page is given from Moulton's *History of the English Bible.*

[2] See Eadie, *Hist. Eng. Bible,* vol. i. p. 383.

[3] "Biblia—the Bible: that is the Holy Scripture of the Olde and Newe Testament faithfully and truly translated out of Douche and Latyn in to Englishe MDXXXV."

his version is its pure, strong English idiom, sometimes quaint withal, but generally musical. Some of the most rhythmical and familiar passages in the Psalms come to us from Coverdale's Version. He also edited a New Testament, 1538, with the Latin and English side by side.

14. *Matthew's Bible*, 1537, which was issued soon after Coverdale's, and before the Great Bible, was the reputed work of *Thomas Matthew*. But this was clearly an assumed name, and it is almost certain that the real author was *John Rogers* the martyr. Rogers was a friend of Tyndale, and the translation is substantially the version of Tyndale except from Ezra to Malachi, which is almost identical with Coverdale's, 1535.

15. *Taverner's Bible, 1539*, is a comparatively unimportant revision of Matthew's Bible, the chief difference in the Old Testament consisting in the omission or abridgment of the notes. In the New Testament changes were made in the text also, some of them valuable; but his version is of unequal merit. As a scholar Richard Taverner was capricious.

16. TYNDALE'S NEW TESTAMENT VERSION, 1526.—When a learned papist declared with some zeal to William Tyndale, "We were better be without God's law than the pope's," Tyndale replied, "If God spare my life, ere many years I will cause a ploughboy to know more of the Scripture than thou doest." Though he died a martyr, 1536, he was able to fulfill his declaration. But he was compelled to leave England in 1524 and completed his translation in exile.

17. *Tyndale's New Testament, 1526*, was the first English version made directly from the Greek, (since Wycliffe's version was from the Latin Vulgate), and the first

The xiij. Chapter.

The same daye went Jesus out of the housse/and satt by the see syde/and mo= the people resorted vnto him/so gretly that he wet and satt in a shyppe/and all the people stode on the shoare. And he spake many thyngs to them in similituds/ saynge: beholde/the sower went forth to sowe/— — — —

¶ And hys disciples cam/and sayde to him: Why speakest thou to them in parables: he answered and saide vnto them: hit is geven vnto you to knowe the secrett of the kyngdo= me of heven/but to them it is nott geven. For whosumever hath/to him shall hit be geven: and he shall have aboundan= nce: But whosoever hath nott: from him shalbe taken a waye eve that same that he hath. Therfore speake I to them in similituds: For though they se/they se nott: and hearynge they heare not: nether vnderstonde. And in them ys fulfylled the prophesy of esay/which prophesi sayth: with youre eares ye shall heare/and shall not vnderstonde/and with youre eyes ye shall se/and shall not perceave. For this peoples hert ys

De that hath, whe re the worde of god is vnderstode / the re hit multiplieth/z makith the people better, where hit is not vnderstode/th' eare hit decreasith I makith the people woorse.

mat. iiij.
Lu. v.viij.

mat.xro

esa.vi.

English New Testament printed.[1] It was issued at Worms in two editions, a quarto and an octavo; 3000 copies of each were printed and sent to England in the spring of 1526. The title-page has an illuminated border showing figures of the four Evangelists and the Apostles Peter, Paul, James and Jude; but it gives no clue to editor, printer, place or date of publication.

18. *Its Chief Features.*—The version is vigorous, clear and simple enough in style for the " ploughboy " to understand. The text is arranged in paragraphs, with chapter divisions but no verses. It omits the doxology to the Lord's Prayer. Tyndale also translated various portions of the Old Testament, including all of the Pentateuch, which were published after his death. Tyndale's work was revised and incorporated into *Matthew's Bible,* 1537, as already stated.

19. Our Common Version is more deeply indebted for its felicities of language to Tyndale's than to any other version. "Our English Testament," says Ellicott, "after all its changes, revisions and remodellings, is still truly and substantially the venerable version of Tyndale the martyr."[2] "The peculiar genius," says Froude, "which breathes through it [our English Bible], the mingled tenderness and majesty—the Saxon simplicity—the preternatural grandeur—unequalled, unapproached in the attempted improvements of modern scholars, all are here, and bear the impress of the mind of one man—William Tyndale."[3]

20. WYCLIFFE'S VERSION, 1382, was the first complete

---

[1] The only portion of the Scriptures printed in English before this was a portion of the Psalms, in 1505.

[2] On Revision, p. 85.

[3] *Hist. Eng.,* vol. iii. p. 84.

translation of the Bible into English.[1] But it was made from the Latin Vulgate, and as it was before the invention of the art of printing, it was a manuscript or written Bible. This translation of the New Testament was completed in 1380, and was entirely by John de Wycliffe or Wiclif.[2] The Old Testament was finished about 1382, Nicholas de Hereford aiding Wycliffe in this portion of the work.

21. A careful revision, called *Purvey's Version*, has several important changes, and as a marked feature, short comments in the margin. These versions are anonymous. A translator of the Bible was exposed to peril, making concealment necessary. But the versions were not hid. They were eagerly sought and read. Copies were made and passed into the hands of all classes of people. The king and the princes had them. Nearly 170 manuscript copies of Purvey's Version made before 1430 have been preserved and examined, although a strict inquisition in that age searched for and burned all the writings of Wycliffe and his followers which could be found. Of the character of this first English Bible it must be said that it was baldly

---

[1] Metrical versions and paraphrases of portions of the Bible were made in English earlier than Wycliffe, and two prose versions of the Psalms, one by William of Shoreham, 1327, and the other soon after by Richard Rolle. Foxe, Johnson, Newcome and others, including Sir Thomas More, have asserted that Bede translated the Scriptures complete into the vernacular; but their assertion is not supported by history. More appears to have referred to portions of the Bible rendered into Anglo-Saxon, and the statements of others rest upon mistaken information. See George P. Marsh, Lects. Eng. Lang.; Preface to Wyckliffe by Forshall and Madden.

[2] His name was spelled about thirty different ways, giving an excellent illustration of the unsettled condition of the English tongue at that period.

A copy of the Bible in 1429 cost from £2 to £3, and for a few leaves poor persons gladly gave a load of hay.

I wyll prayse the D lorde/ that though thou
wast turned/ and thou hast comforte
me. Beholde God is my saluacion: I wyll be
bolde therfore and not feare. For the lorde
God is my strength and my prayse to be of
I synge: and is become my saluacion. And ye
shall drawe water in gladnes oute of the wel
les of saluacion. And ye shall saye in that da:
ye: geue thankes unto the lorde/ call on his na
me: make his dedes knowen amonge the pe=
ople: remember that his name is hie. Lyfte
up. Synge unto the lorde/ for he hath done
excellentlye/ and that is knowen thorow ou=
te all the worlde. Crye and showte thou in=
habiter of Sion/ for great amonge you is the
holye of Israel.

ISAIAH, CHAP. XII.: TYNDALE (1534).

FAC-SIMILE OF EARLY ENGLISH MANUSCRIPT BIBLES.

SPECIMEN OF ANGLO-SAXON VERSION FROM THE RUSHWORTH GOSPELS: JOHN 13:2. The line in large letters is Latin, with the Anglo-Saxon equivalents in the line above.

literal. Yet, thrown into modern forms of spelling, the version has many words and phrases that were retained in later translations. It was the language of the people, and fed their hungry souls with the bread from God.

22. *Anglo-Saxon Versions.*—Most of the translations of portions of the Bible, earlier than Wycliffe' s, were mere paraphrases, sometimes failing to give the correct sense of Scripture. Such a paraphrase of the Gospels and the Acts in English, but written in the Saxon characters, was made in the latter half of the twelfth century by Orme or Ormun, and is called the "Ormulum." Several interlinear versions (Vulgate of Jerome and the Vernacular) were made in the tenth and eleventh centuries, a part of one known as the "Rushworth Gloss" being now in the Bodleian library. These interlinear versions were probably made for the use of priests who did not understand the Latin. King Alfred made a translation of the Ten Commandments, portions of the Gospels, and he projected a translation of the Psalter, but his death prevented its completion. The Venerable Bede

(672–755) completed a translation of the Gospel of John into the vernacular and wrote commentaries on most of the books of the Bible. His Church History was among the first books printed in Germany (1474). The earliest Anglo-Saxon paraphrases of portions of the Bible were in verse, by Guthloe, Aldhelm, and the most noted one by Cædmon, about 680. The Christian Scriptures were reputed to have been introduced into England by the Monk Augustin, about 596, who used copies of the Old Latin Version, from which the earlier Anglo-Saxon translations were made.

23. *Language of English Bible.*—(1) In many paragraphs of the common English Version 39 words in 40 are of Anglo-Saxon derivation.

(2) In the story of Joseph (Gen. 42 : 21–29), there are only 7 words beside proper names which are not Anglo-Saxon.

(3) In the parable of the Sower (Matt. 13, etc.), of 106 different words, only 3 are not Anglo-Saxon.

(4) The Lord's Prayer (Matt. 6 : 9–13) has 65 words ("forever" one word), 59 are of Anglo-Saxon and 6 are of Latin derivation.

(5) In John 11 : 32–36, 70 words in 72 are of Anglo-Saxon origin. In Milton's "Paradise Lost," Book IV : 639, etc., of 90 words only 74 are Anglo-Saxon. In the famous passage of Shakespeare, "To be or not to be," of 81 words 13 are not Anglo-Saxon. This shows the great comparative strength of the English Bible in words of Anglo-Saxon origin.

24. *Leading Facts about English Bibles.*

(1) First complete Bible in English (by Wycliffe) *from the Latin,* 1382.

(2) First complete New Testament in English (by Tyndale) *from the Greek*, 1526.

(3) First *printed* English Bible, complete (Coverdale's), 1535.

(4) First English Testament divided into verses (Genevan), 1557.

(5) First English Bible divided into verses (Genevan), 1560.

(6) First English Bible, translated complete from the original languages, Greek and Hebrew (the Genevan Version), 1560.

(7) Cost of early English Bibles: two arches of the London bridge, built in the thirteenth century, are reported to have cost £25; a written copy of the Bible cost £30. A laborer's wages was 1½d. a day and board; hence the cost of a Bible would be equal to a laborer's wages for about fifteen years. It was perilous for common people to read or to own a Bible. For example, in 1429, Marjery Backster was indicted for asking her maid to hear her husband read the Bible by night. In 1514–1519, John Stevenson was arrested for teaching the Ten Commandments, and Thomas Collins had his father arrested for the same offence. Robert Pope informed against his wife, son and father for hearing the Gospel of Matthew read to them.

CHAPTER III.

1. Next to a knowledge of our own versions, all English-speaking peoples should gain some knowledge of the German versions of the Bible. While the Common Version of the English Bible is the growth of centuries, the mature fruit of successive generations of Biblical scholars from Wyckliffe to the King James revisers, the German version bears largely the impress of one mind and one genius—Martin Luther. There were earlier versions in German, but the great version, the one version and the only popular one that is truly German, is that made by the great reformer.

2. *Earlier German Versions.*—Passing the Gothic version of the fourth century, there was a translation of the Bible made in the fourteenth century, by some unknown scholars,[1] from the Latin Vulgate. No less than seventeen editions of it were printed between 1462 and 1522—fourteen of them in High German and three or four in Low German dialect. Most of these were issued of folio size, in two volumes, with wood engravings. The Archbishop of Mainz in 1486 forbade the printing of sacred and learned books, especially the German Bible, on the ground that the German language was incapable of correctly rep-

---

[1] Some have ascribed the earlier German version to the Waldenses (Keller, Haupt), but it may have sprung from a love of the word within the Romish Church (Jostes, Schaff and others). In the Munich Library are twenty-one *written* copies of the Gospels and Epistles in early German versions.

resenting religious ideas and the profound sense of Greek and Latin works !

3. *Luther's Version.*—While Luther was held a willing prisoner in Wartburg Castle, he translated the New Testament into German, and it was published in 1522. Its title was "Das Newe Testament Deutzsch. Wittemberg." It was illustrated with wood engravings by the famous Lucas Cranach, having one illustration at the beginning of each book and twenty-one in the book of Revelation. It was divided into chapters like the Latin Bible, and into paragraphs, but not into verses. The Pentateuch appeared in 1523, the Psalms in 1524, and the entire Bible (including the Apocrypha) in 1534. In translating the Old Testament, Luther formed a committee (Bible club) of his colleagues, Melanchthon, Justus Jonas and four others, who aided him in the work. Luther continued to amend and improve the version, issuing five successive revisions of it, the last in 1545. He retained a Latin form of title, *Biblia*, and the translation was issued in folio, with numerous engravings.

4. *Merits of Luther's Version.*—The German Bible was received with great enthusiasm. A hundred thousand copies—an enormous number for that age—were sold between 1534 and 1574.[1] If his version did not form, it may be said to have reformed, unified and crystallized the German language. It gave it wings, and made it intelligible to the common people in all parts of Germany. It is the first great German classic. It brought one language out of many dialects—the language afterward of the golden era of German literature, the speech of Lessing, Herder, Goethe and Schiller.[2]

---

[1] See Schaff, *Hist. Christ. Ch.*, vol. vi. p. 350.
[2] Heinrich Heine, the poet, critic and German Voltaire, says of

5. *The original text* of the New Testament, upon which Luther based his version, was the Greek text edited by Erasmus, 1519. The Old Testament was translated from the Massoretic Hebrew text, edited by G. Ben Moseh, 1494; but the Septuagint and the Latin Vulgate were often consulted, and in the Apocrypha the latter was chiefly used as a basis.[1]

6. *Revisions of Luther's Version.*—Besides Luther's own revisions of his version, there have been many others, the most important being an official revision ordered by the Eisenach German Evangelical Conference of 1863. This was completed and published at Halle in 1883, and is known as the *Probebibel.* The revision was made by a company of eminent Biblical scholars (eleven on the New Testament and twenty on the Old Testament), among whom were Tholuck, Riehm, Schlottmann, Dillmann, Delitzsch, Meyer, Dorner and Köstlin. The revision was extremely conservative, but was so sharply criticised that the Eisenach Conference of 1886 recommitted it for final action. While German scholars are bold and independent in theology, they are conservative and timid in questions of translation affecting the laity.

7. The Roman Catholics, though stoutly opposed to giving the people the Bible in the vernacular, were compelled

---

Luther, " He created the German language. He did this by his translation of the Bible."—*Hist. of Religion and Poetry in Germany*, London, vol. i. pp. 425, 427.

[1] Luther omitted the famous text respecting the three heavenly witnesses, 1 John 5 : 7, which appears first in the Frankfort edition of Luther's version (from Erasmus' Greek text of 1522), and is retained in the revised version of Luther, 1883, but is placed in brackets. The most popular text of Luther's Bible is that by the Canstein Bible Society.

by Luther's work to issue rival versions in self-defence.[1]
The chief German versions by Romanists were by Emser,
1527, Dietenberger, 1534, and Eck, 1537. They are all
from the Vulgate, and generally clumsy and stiff, lacking
the purity of German idiom which is found in Luther's
version.   Dietenberger's revision has been revised by Ulen-
berg, 1630, and re-revised by theologians of Mainz, 1662,
and since been issued as the Catholic Bible used in Germany and by German Catholics.   Among German versions
or translations of the Bible made for scholars, that by De
Wette, 1809, 4th ed. 1858, and that of Weizsäcker, Tübin-
gen, 1875, are the best.

8. *Dutch Versions.*—The first complete translation of the
Bible into Dutch was made by Jacob Van Liesveldt, and
issued in two volumes folio, Antwerp, 1526. The second
edition cost the printer his head. The version was partially supplanted by Utenhove's version in 1556. These
versions were not in the best idiomatic Dutch. The first
was based on Luther's version and the Cologne Bible ; the
second upon Luther's German and Olivetan's French
version.

9. A new version was ordered by the Dutch synod in
1571 ; but owing to troubles and divisions in affairs, and to
the deaths of scholars, the work was twice interrupted and
long delayed. It was again ordered by the famous Synod
of Dort, 1618, which appointed three translators and fourteen revisers ; but the new order was not approved by the
States General until 1624, and the work was begun in 1626
and was carried on at Leyden for eleven years. The new

---

[1] Emser charged Luther with a thousand grammatical and heretical
errors, four being in the Lord's Prayer; among them, that he added
the doxology, which is not in the Latin Vulgate.

translation finally appeared in two editions—one with and one without marginal readings and references—in 1637. It is called the *States' Bible;* and so superior was its merit that within fifteen years it gained unanimous popular favor and ecclesiastical approval. It is remarkable for its felicity of expression, and scholars regard it as one of the best of existing versions.

10. The General Synod appointed a committee of fourteen, in 1854, to revise the old translation, in view of the progress in Biblical criticism. The New Testament revision was completed and issued in 1867, but its reception was not hearty; indeed it was so adverse that the Old Testament part was indefinitely postponed.

11. *French Versions.*—Pierre, about 1170, made a Bible History in French, and Gruars, in 1286–89, prepared a similar French Bible History. The first complete French version of the Bible was by Jean de Rely, a Roman Catholic, in 1487, based on the Vulgate and former partial versions. There were twelve editions of this version issued. Another version was made by Lefèvre d'Etaples, and issued in Antwerp, 1530. Pierre Robert Olivetan with the aid of that version made another, corrected by Calvin, issued at the expense of the Waldenses in 1535, which is known as the first Protestant version. The evangelical pastors of Geneva appointed a company from their own number (among them Beza) to issue a new version, which was completed in 1588. This version was revised by Martin, Amsterdam, 1707, and by Ostervald, 1724.

12. Louis Segond issued a new version, Geneva, 1874, third ed. 1879, being a direct translation from Hebrew and Greek into French. This version is printed by the Oxford press (fifty thousand copies first edition), with prose text in

paragraphs and the poetry in verse form, the verses being noted in the margin. It also has brief notes and prefaces to the books, and is regarded as a decided improvement upon all previous French versions. The British and Foreign Bible Society, however, circulates the older versions by Martin and Ostervald, revised by the Bible Society of France.

13. *Italian Versions.*—There were several translations of the Bible into Italian before the Reformation, the more important being that of Nicolo, Venice, 1471, and of Bruccioli from the original texts—New Testament, 1530, the entire Bible, Venice, 1532. The latter translator was indignant at the prohibition of the spread of the Bible among the people in the vernacular, but his version was put , first in a Roman Catholic list of prohibited books.

14. The first Protestant version of the Bible complete in Italian appeared in Geneva, 1562, but was displaced by that of Deodati, made from the original texts, Geneva, 1607, in the Lucchese dialect and suited for the peasants. Another version by Martini, Roman Catholic Archbishop of Florence, made from a version of the Latin, was issued at Turin, 1776, and is circulated by the British and Foreign Bible Society (New Testament, ed. 1813, the Bible, ed. 1821), along with the versions of Deodati and others.

15. *Spanish Versions.*—The earliest known translation of the New Testament into Spanish is that of Francisco, issued at Antwerp, 1543, and by Juan Perez, Venice, 1556. The whole Bible was translated by Cassidoro Regno and published at Basel, 1569 ; was revised by Valera and issued at Amsterdam, 1602. Another version was made by San Miguel and published at Madrid, in 1794. This was in nineteen volumes, and had the Latin and Spanish texts and

3

a commentary by the translator.   The British and Foreign Bible Society has distributed Valera's and San Miguel's versions (the text only) since 1828 until the present (1891).

16. *Danish Versions.*—The first complete Danish version of the Bible was edited under the name of C. Pederson in 1550, and has been often revised, a thorough revision being made in 1815 to 1824, which is still circulated by the British and Foreign Bible Society along with a recent revision, and a special revision known as the Norwegian Bible, made by the Norwegian Bible Society and a committee of revision appointed in 1871.   Until the division of the kingdoms, in 1814, the Norwegians used the ordinary Danish version.

17. A *Swedish version* was completed in 1541 by Laurentius and Olaus Petri.   This has been often revised and is still in use.

18. Besides the versions in the principal languages of Europe, there have been many versions and revisions made in   other European languages and dialects, as the Welsh, Gaelic, Irish, Portuguese, Lap, Polish, Bohemian, Russ, Slavonic, Modern Greek and many others.   Of these, and the two hundred to three hundred missionary translations, particular notice cannot here be given.

19. The modern *Arabic version* begun by Eli Smith, 1847, and completed by his co-laborer, C. V. A. Van Dyck, 1866, is a monument of patient, persevering and profound scholarship.   It is accounted one of the most faithful and finished of all modern missionary versions.

CHAPTER IV.

1. One book of religion—the Bible—has been valued and loved by the learned and unlearned, by priest and people, for more than eighteen centuries. No other sacred book has been so deeply or so widely endeared to the human heart. There is no other book with a history like that of the Bible. In the early centuries of Christianity, translations of the Bible into the vernacular or common speech of the peoples were made and circulated wherever the gospel gained a foothold among a nation or a people. Several of the more important of these translations, or portions of them, have been preserved to our times, and are of value in establishing the early and often the true reading of the original copy of the Christian Scriptures. Some of these versions will now be briefly described.

2. *The Armenian.*—The gospel was introduced into Armenia from Cappadocia; and the translations of the Bible into Armenian were probably made from Greek manuscripts obtained from some portion of Asia Minor. At first the Armenian disciples may have used Syriac copies of the Scriptures; but early in the fourth century they had a written language, formed from an alphabet of thirty-six letters. The earliest version of the Scriptures in Armenian appears to have been made from the Peshito (Syriac). Later in

(43)

that century (431 to 450) a new translation, direct from
the Greek, was suggested by Miesrob and Moses Chorenen-
sis, and was completed by two scholars, Joseph and Eznak,
who went to Alexandria to perfect their knowledge of the
Greek. The existing manuscripts of this version are not
very ancient, but they contain the entire Bible. The best
printed edition is by Zohrab, and is now issued by the
British and Foreign Bible Society.

3. *The Gothic.*—The Goths, in their old home about
Mœsia, were early led to accept Christianity. Their second bishop, Ulphilas (Ulfilas or Wulfilas), 348 A. D.,
though an Arian, translated the Bible (except I., II. Sam.
and I., II. Kings) from Greek into Gothic. The gospels are
placed in the " western " order, that is, Matthew, John,
Luke, Mark. Seven manuscripts containing portions of
this version have been preserved ; but they are fragmentary,
large gaps occurring and missing leaves in both the Old
and New Testament portions. The best-printed editions
are: A. Uppström, Upsala, 1854–1868, and E. Bernhardt,
Halle, 1875,—the latter being the Gothic and Greek, with
critical notes.

4. *The Coptic or Egyptian Versions.*—Little has been
definitely known of these ancient Coptic translations until
recently. Three are known in three different dialects: (1)
The *Memphitic* or *Bahiric* dialect of lower Egypt. This
translation belongs to the second century. There are in
the various libraries of Europe twenty-eight manuscript
copies of the Gospels in the Memphitic dialect, seventeen
copies of the Pauline and catholic Epistles and the Acts
(the Acts follow instead of precede the Epistles), and ten
of the book of Revelation. This translation is regarded
as of great importance, because it is believed to indicate

the text current at Alexandria, free from many corruptions prevailing in the second century. (2) The *Thebaic* or *Sahidic* version, in the dialect of upper Egypt, also exists in manuscripts, but only in a very fragmentary form.[1] The best-printed edition of the Thebaic translation is by C. G. Woide, completed by Ford, Oxford, 1799. (3) The *Bashmuric* or *Eleaarchian* translation, probably belonging to the third century, of which only fragments of John's Gospel and of the Pauline Epistles have been found. This version is based upon the Thebaic, the Bashmuric being a modification of the Thebaic dialect, and the Bashmuric translation is chiefly useful in texts where the Thebaic is wanting.

5. *An Ethiopic version* was early made for use in Abyssinia, probably in the fourth century. The manuscript copies of this version are not very ancient ; but the Ethiopic has now given place to a later dialect, the Amharic, into which the Bible has been translated.

6. *The Syriac Versions.*—The Syriac or Aramæan belongs to the Semitic family of languages, and is older than the patriarch Jacob. It is copious, flexible and dignified, and the Old and New Testaments were translated into that tongue and used in public worship from the second century downward.

---

[1] These ancient Coptic translations show that the books then included in the New Testament were the same as now, except the Apocalypse. The order, however, was different; the four Gospels were first, but usually in this order—John, Matthew, Mark, Luke; then came the Pauline Epistles, including that to the Hebrews, next the catholic or general epistles, and lastly Acts. In some of the manuscripts the book of Revelation appears at the end; but there are lectionaries or Scripture service lessons between the book of Acts and the book of Revelation. This would indicate that Revelation was not admitted to the New Testament in the opinion of those who made the

7. There are four versions in Syriac :—(1) The *Peshito* (*Pĕ-shĭt'-to*), (or Peshitto, Peschito, or Peshitta), meaning "simple" or faithful, so called from the character of the version. In its present form it belongs to the third or fourth century. It has been known to scholars for over three centuries.[1] (2) The *Curetorian* is a fragment of the Gospels, but now generally conceded to be the earliest of all versions in Syriac. It was found in a convent in the desert, seventy miles northwest of Cairo, in 1842, and published, with an English translation by Dr. Cureton, in 1858, and with three added leaves (1871) by J. R. Crowfoot in Greek, London, 1870–72. (3) The *Philoxenian* or *Harklean* was a Syriac version made in the fifth century by Xenias or Philoxenus, a heretical bishop of eastern Syria. It was carefully revised by Thomas of Harkel or Heraclea, 616, who compared it with some ancient Greek copies. The best existing manuscript of this version is from Mardin, and belongs to the Protestant College at Beirut. (4) The *Jerusalem Syriac* is an evangelistary, or selections from the Gospels, found in five existing manuscripts in the Vatican at Rome. The version belongs to the fifth century.

8. *The Latin.*—The ancient versions of the Bible in Latin may be classed in two groups :—(1) *Old Latin;* (2) The *Vulgate,* by Jerome, in its varied recensions. The Old Latin translation was known to the Latin fathers, as Tertullian, Cyprian, the two Hilarys, Ambrose, Jerome, Augustine, Pelagius and others. It dates back to the mid-

---

translation, or else that it belonged to a *second* canon, as we know was the case for a time with some of the shorter epistles.

[1] The best printed edition in England is by the British and Foreign Bible Society, and by Bagster. A better American edition is by Dr. J. Perkins, Oroomiah, 1841, and New York, 1874; also a literal translation from the Syriac Peshito, by Dr. Murdock, New York, 1857.

dle or latter half of the second century. It was made from the Septuagint, in the Old Testament, and is in the rough Latin of the second century, which lacks classic polish, yet is not without vigor and terseness of expression.

9. Fragments of the Old Latin translations are still extant, and indicate three variant types of the text—an African, a European, and one of the character which Augustine commends as the Itala. Whether all these forms are based upon one African translation or on different independent translations is an unsettled question. This much seems to be generally agreed by the best critics, that the earliest form of the Old Latin version is of north African origin. From thirty to forty manuscripts of portions of the Old Latin version are known to be in existence. A carefully-edited and printed edition of these Old Latin versions, in a satisfactory form for general use among scholars, is a thing desired.

10. *The Vulgate.*—Jerome, one of the most learned men of. his time, urged by the Roman bishop Damasus, about 383 A.D., undertook a thorough revision of the Old Latin versions, that he might make a Vulgate (Vulgata) or Latin text of the Bible which would be universally accepted by Latin-speaking peoples. His work of revising the Old Latin versions led Jerome to undertake a new and more faithful translation of the Old Testament from the Hebrew. He spent about twenty years (385 to 405) at Bethlehem, the town in which our Saviour was born, in these labors.[1] Jerome's version was not at first regarded with favor; but after some years its superior merit brought it into general

---

[1] At Bethlehem, in the crypt under the Church of the Nativity, is a room called the "Chapel of St. Jerome," in which this great man is said to have pursued his studies and work of translating the Bible.

use. For years it raised a howl of indignation. Jerome was irritated by the attacks of the ignorant priests, whom he calls *bipedes asellos*, "two-legged donkeys." Long after Jerome's death his version was accepted, and 1000 years later was counted superior to the original text ! The Latin Bible which came thus into use as Jerome's version was in fact a composite work. The Old Testament, excepting the Psalms, was from his new translation made from the Hebrew. The Psalms were his revision of the Old Latin, based not upon the original Hebrew but upon the Septuagint.[1] The Apocrypha was also from the Old Latin translation, excepting the two books of Judith and Tobit, which were from Jerome's new version. The New Testament books were revised from the Old Latin version. The text became so corrupt that Charlemagne about 802 directed Alcuin to collate the copies and revise the Latin text.

11. The Council of Trent, 1546, decreed what books were to be received as canonical, and that the text of the Latin edition was authentic. But the question at once arose, Which Latin text, and which edition of it, is the authentic one ? Pope Sixtus V. issued a revised edition of the Vulgate text in 1590, which he decreed to be the authoritative edition, and threatened excommunication against any who used any other. Sixtus died that year. So many errors, however, were pointed out in the Sixtine edition that Bellarmin proposed to issue a corrected edition in Sixtus' name, and this pious fraud was actually undertaken, and in the new edition all the principal blunders in the

---

[1] It was called the *Roman Psalter*, while Jerome's new translation was known as the *Gallican Psalter*. The former was retained in the Latin Bibles until Pius V., 1566, when it was displaced by the *Gallican Psalter*.

former edition were charged to the printers! Clement
VIII. had the new edition of the Latin text prepared with
greater care and issued in 1592, in the face of the threatened anathema of his predecessor, Sixtus V.[1]   This Clementine text is the standard Roman Catholic Bible, taking
precedence in that church of the Hebrew and Greek original texts in questions of doctrine and life.   A critical edition of Jerome's Latin version is wanting, though the
materials for it are abundant.

12. *The Septuagint*, or Greek version of the Old Testament, was made by Hellenistic Jews of Alexandria, between 285 and 247 B.C.   According to Jewish tradition, it
was made by seventy or seventy-two elders (hence its title;
Septuaginta, or seventy) sent from Jerusalem; but great
obscurity rests upon the real time and history of its origin.[2]
It is also very difficult now to ascertain *precisely* what was
the reading of the original Septuagint, but it is assumed
that the text we have is in the main that current in the days
of our Lord.   From this version Jesus quotes, and so do
the apostles.   It was the accepted Scriptures of the dis-
persed Jews, and is the basis of the Greek used by early
Christian writers.   The Septuagint is in the main faithful to
the Hebrew text, although it cannot be said to be minutely
accurate, judged by the Hebrew now current, and some-

---

[1] These are known as the Sixtine or Clementine Latin texts.

[2] The importance of this translation is apparent not merely from its
great antiquity, which, between conflicting Hebrew readings, indicates
the one then current, but also from the fact that of 290 direct quotations from the Old Testament in the New, the great majority agree better with the Septuagint than with the Hebrew.   More exactly, according to Turpie, 90 quotations agree with the Septuagint, of which 53
also agree with the Hebrew; 10 agree with the Hebrew but not with
the Septuagint; 175 differ from both, but these generally are nearer to
the Septuagint than to the Hebrew.

times gives a paraphrase rather than a close translation of
the Hebrew text.   It was freely used by the early Christian
fathers.   The current text of the Greek Scriptures had become corrupted from frequent copying during several
centuries.   In order to attain a better text, Origen (184–
254) edited a *tetrapla*, or fourfold text, and later on his
hexapla, or sixfold Bible text.   In the first he arranged in
parallel columns the Hebrew, the Septuagint and three
other Greek versions made in the second century by Aquila,
Symmachus and Theodotion.   In the latter he added three
anonymous Greek translations, numbered fifth, sixth and
seventh, all in parallel columns in order to show the true
reading and meaning of the Hebrew Scriptures.[1]

13. THE TARGUMS is the general term for the Chaldee or
Aramaic versions and paraphrases of portions of the Old
Testament.   Eight are now extant, of which three are
upon the Pentateuch, two on Esther, and others upon the
prophets, poetical books and other portions of the Old
Testament.   These are generally very free translations, and
often diffuse paraphrases.   The so-called Targum of Onke-
los on the Pentateuch and of *Jerushalmi* in its first form
are the most literal versions.   These works were a growth
from oral traditions and teachings, and of great interest to
Old Testament students.   The earliest historic instance of
a targum is when Ezra read the law to the returned exiles,
and the scribes were compelled to "give the sense and

---

[1] Aquila was a Jewish proselyte of Pontus, who made a Greek version of the Hebrew Scriptures, 117-138 A.D., to use in discussions with
the Christians, because the Septuagint version was used against the
Jews.   Theodotion made a revision of the Greek version of the Old
Testament about the same period as the work by Aquila, and his version is retained in Greek Bibles.   The version by Symmachus, an
Ebionite disciple, was made somewhat later.

cause them to understand the reading,'' Neh. 8 : 8 From
these interpretations the targums grew.   Their present
written form does not date earlier than the second century
of our era.   They were written in the later Hebrew dialect,
the Aramaic.

CHAPTER V.

1. *How Written.*—The oldest existing copies of the books of the New Testament, in their original Greek, are written upon fine *vellum*, made from the skins of very young calves. Some are written upon *parchment*, made from the skins of sheep or goats.

The Sinaitic MS. is made of fine skins of antelopes. The leaves of this MS. are so large that the skin of one antelope would make only two leaves. As the MS. in its present fragmentary state has 346½ leaves, and, adding the 43 previously discovered, 389½ leaves, it must have required 195 antelopes to make the vellum on which it is written! The Vatican MS. is written upon vellum admired by all who have seen it, for the beauty of its finish and texture. It is supposed that earlier copies of the New Testament books were written upon less durable papyrus, and hence have perished. The manuscript copies of the New Testament are older than any existing written copies of the Old Testament in Hebrew; but the oldest MSS. of the New Testament contain the whole or large portions of the Old Testament in Greek.

2. *Classes.*—These ancient MSS. of the New Testament may be classified:

I. By their contents, as (1) those containing the whole

of the New Testament ; (2) copies containing portions only ; (3) those having church lessons.

II. By their supposed age, as (1) those of the fourth century (the oldest now known); (2) of the fifth century ; (3) of the sixth century, and so on.

Or, III. By the style of the writing, as, (1) *Uncials*, that is those written in capitals ; (2) *Cursives*, that is, those written in a running hand.

More recently they have also been classified by critical scholars according to their genealogical origin, or the source from which the text of each MS. was derived. Thus MSS. of the New Testament are divided into Alexandrian, Western and Neutral groups, to which may be added the Syrian ; there are mixed readings in older MSS. as in the versions before 250 A. D.

3. *The number* of uncial MSS. of the New Testament now known is about 110, and of cursives over 3500. Scrivener (1883) noted 97 uncials, and 1997 cursives; Abbot (1885) 92 uncials, and 1600 cursives; Schaff (1888) 91 uncials. But Gregory (Suppl't to N. T. 1890) noted 87 uncials, described 22 new ones, making 109 uncials, and gives a table of 3553 cursive manuscripts.

4. DIVISIONS OF THE TEXT.—In the earliest manuscripts there are no spaces between the words, and no marks between sentences except an occasional dot at the top of the line. But there are divisions into paragraphs, and marks indicating sections. For example, in the Gospels there are numerals marking and dividing the text of Matthew into 170 unequal sections, Mark into 62, Luke into 150 and John into 80. Similar sections, though not as ancient, are found in the Acts and Epistles.

5. *Titloi.*—In other MSS. of the fifth century and later

there are divisions into sections or chapters, called τίτλοι = *titloi*, as the title of the section is given with its number. These differ from the former divisions, for in the Gospels they uniformly begin with what we would regard as the *second* section. The general title to the book was apparently sufficient to designate the *first* section. Of these *titloi* = titles, Matthew has 68, Mark 48, Luke 83 and John 18. There was a similar division of the Acts and Epistles into "headings" or chapters, of a later origin.

6. *The Ammonian or Eusebian sections* of the Gospels was another and different grouping, made to facilitate the finding of the different passages that were parallel in the four Gospels; hence some were long and some very short. John 19 : 6, for example, is divided into three sections. These sections were numbered in the margin consecutively from the beginning of each Gospel. Matthew had 355 such sections, Mark (originally) 233, Luke 342 and John 232. Eusebius divided the numbers of these sections into ten tables or "canons." The first, in four columns, notes the sections that are parallel in all four Gospels; the next three, the sections that are parallel in three of the Gospels; the next five tables note the sections parallel in two of the Gospels; the last table gives the sections peculiar to each Gospel.

7. *Modern Divisions.*—These ancient divisions of the New Testament text and similar divisions of the text of the Old Testament, coupled with the necessity for some division to facilitate ready and accurate reference, led to the modern division of the Bible into chapters and verses. The chapter divisions in our modern Bibles are probably due to Langton, Archbishop of Canterbury (about 1220), and the versicular divisions to Cardinal Hugo (about 1248).* The

---

* But the origin of the versicular divisions is in dispute.

English Revised Version has restored the more ancient method of division of the text into sections or paragraphs, but has preserved the modern chapter-and-verse numerals in the margin.

8. *Uncial Manuscripts.*—Among the most important uncial manuscripts is the *Sinaitic* (known as א), found by Prof. Constantine Tischendorf, in 1859, in the Convent of St. Catherine, on Mount Sinai, and now in the library at St. Petersburg, Russia. It contains the whole of the New Testament in Greek, the Epistle of Barnabas and part of the Shepherd of Hermas, and a large part of the Old Tes-

ΤΟΤΗϹΕΥϹΕΒΕΙΑϹ ΜΥϹΤΗΡΙΟΝΟϹΕ

Fourth Cent.   Codex Sinaiticus.—1 Tim. 3 : 16.

το της ευσεβειας | μυστηριον [θε late corr.] ος ε.

tament in the Greek version. It consists of 346½ leaves [1] of very fine thin vellum, 13½ inches long by 14⅞ inches wide. The text is written with four columns of 48 lines each on a page, except in the poetical books of the Old Testament, which have but two columns on a page. The words have no spaces between them, and are often abbreviated by a line over the letters. There are corrections or alterations by later hands in succession, noticeable from the different form of the letters and different shades of inks, so that Prof. Tischendorf distinguished the work of ten different correctors. A fac-simile edition of the MS. was printed at the expense of the emperor of Russia, and

---

[1] To these are to be added 43 leaves found in 1844 and called *Codex Friderico-Augustanus*, and two leaves and a fragment of a leaf found in 1853 and belonging originally to this Sinaitic MS., making in all upwards of 391 ½ leaves.

about a dozen copies came to the United States, to several important libraries, as the Astor, Lenox and American Bible Society libraries. The MS. belongs to the fourth century, and Tischendorf supposed it might be one of the fifty copies which Constantine had prepared in 331 A. D.

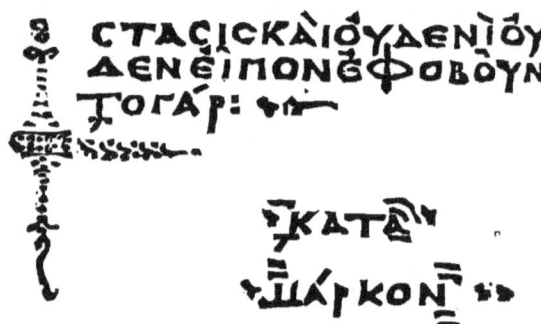

Fourth Cent. Codex Vaticanus.—Mark 16 : 8.
στασις και ουδενι ου | δεν ειπον εφοβουν | το γαρ :

9. The *Vatican manuscript* (known as B) also belongs to the fourth century, and contains most of the Old Testament in Greek and the New Testament to Heb. 9 : 14. It is written on fine vellum, in three columns of 42 lines each to a page. It has 759 leaves, 10 by 10½ inches, and is perhaps more carefully written than the Sinaitic MS. It is believed to have been copied in Egypt, and was brought to Rome in 1448. Early in this century it was for a time in Paris, but was soon restored to Rome, and is kept in the Vatican library. This MS. also shows numerous corrections by different hands. Several editions of it have been printed : Tischendorf's, Vercellone and Cozza's, and the best, a photographic facsimile, 1890–91. There is another Vatican MS. B (No. 2066), containing the Book of Revelation, which is of later origin and belongs to the eighth

century. The Vatican MS. is of the first importance in critical study of the New Testament text ; and the Sinaitic ranks next in value.

10. The *Alexandrian manuscript* was sent from the Patriarch of Constantinople as a present to Charles I. (1628), and was placed in the British Museum, London, in 1753. It is a vellum of 773 leaves, 12¾ by 10¼ inches, each page containing two columns of 50 lines each. It contains nearly the whole of the Old Testament in Greek, and of the New Testament except Matt. 1 to 25 : 26, two leaves from John's Gospel, three from 2 Corinthians, and portions from the edges of the leaves, carelessly cut away in binding, Added to it are the first Epistle of Clement and a part of the sec-

ϹΝΑΡΧΗΗΝΟΛΟΓΟϹΙΚΑΙΟΛΟΓϴϹΗ
ΤΠΓΟϹΤΟΝϴΝΊΚΑΙϴϹΗΝΟΛΟΓΟϹ.

Fifth Cent.   Codex Alexandrinus.—John 1 : 1.

Εν αρχη ην ο λογος και ο λογος ην | προς τον θ[εο]ν: και θ[εο]ς ην ο λογος.

ond also. It was probably written in Alexandria in the fifth century, and has initial letters, and the first four lines of each column of the first page of Genesis in bright vermilion ink. It was among the first of the uncial MSS. used by critical scholars. A photographic fac-simile edition has been published by the British Museum, 1879–82.

11. *The Ephraem manuscript* is in the National Library at Paris, France, and consists of 209 leaves, 64 of the Old Testament in Greek and 145 of the New. It was brought to Florence from the East in the sixteenth century, and is a rescript or palimpsest on vellum ; that is, the old writing (the Bible text) has been partially effaced and some works

4

of Ephraem the Syrian were written over it in the twelfth century. The original writing was known to Wetstein (1716), and edited by Tischendorf (1843–45). Unfortunately, large gaps occur in the New Testament text, so that 37 chapters of the Gospels, 15 of the Acts, 45 chapters of the Epistles and 11 of Revelation are missing. It belongs to the fifth century.

12. The *Greco-Latin manuscript of Beza*, in the Cambridge library, England, contains the Gospels and the Acts. These are written on vellum, one column of 34 lines on a page, the left-hand page presenting the Greek text and the opposite right-hand page having the corresponding Latin version. The great scholar and reformer Theodore Beza says he found the MS. in Lyons (1562), and he gave it to Cambridge University, England, in 1581. The text has many interpolations, and has been boldly altered and corrected by several hands. An edition has been edited in ordinary type by Scrivener (1864), which represents the MS. line for line.

13. *New manuscripts.*—It is quite probable that new manucripts of importance may yet be discovered. A new uncial MS. is reported to have been found (1890) in the Arabic library of Damascus. It is a parchment having 380½ leaves, 12½ by 13¾ inches, and containing the entire New Testament in Greek, part of the Old Testament, and also the Epistle of Barnabas and a portion of the Shepherd of Hermas. The MS. is written with four columns of 50 lines each on a page, and from the description seems like a companion of the famous Sinaitic MS. But we must wait for more definite information about it.

The remaining uncial MSS. are of secondary importance, and do not call for particular description.

14. THE CURSIVES are a numerous class of manuscripts, written in a running hand on vellum or parchment, and some of them on cotton or linen paper. They are often richly illuminated, and date from the ninth to the middle of the fifteenth century, when they were superseded by printed copies of the Bible. About 30 of them are known to contain the entire New Testament ; others have portions; as 600 the Gospels, 300 the Pauline Epistles, 200 the Catholic Epistles, 100 the Book of Revelation, while there are 350 Evangelistaries, that is, "lessons" from the Gospels, and so on. A number have been critically collated, but most of them do not throw any important light upon our present text.

15. HEBREW MANUSCRIPTS.—Written copies of the Hebrew text of the Old Testament are of comparatively recent age, the oldest of the Law not being older than 840 A.D. They have all been written since the period of the Massorites. The rule of the old Talmudists was that all faulty or imperfect MSS. of their sacred books should be destroyed. This may partially account for the scarcity of them. But about fourteen hundred different Hebrew MSS. have been found and examined by Hebrew scholars—chiefly Kennicott and De Rossi.

16. The Hebrew MSS. are of two classes: those prepared for use in the synagogue services, and those intended for private reading. The rules for preparing the manuscript copies of the Old Testament to be used in public worship were many and very strict. The parchment must be made by a Jew, from the skin of an animal that was ceremonially clean. The writing must be in columns exactly equal in length. If more than three words were off the line, the whole work must be thrown aside. It must be

written with a black ink made according to a specific rec-
ipe, and the forms of the letters were minutely specified,
as also the spaces, points and use of the pen. The work
must be carefully revised within thirty days after the copy
was completed, and if then there was a letter wanting in a
word, or if one letter touched another, the manuscript was
condemned. Manuscripts for private use were subject to
less rigorous rules. Although these rules must have been
burdensome to copyists, they were very effective in promot-
ing the preservation of a purer text of the Hebrew Scriptures.

17. *The Hebrew Text.*—It is not easy to determine the
precise reading of the text of the Old Testament for the
reasons already stated. It was formerly supposed that in
Hebrew the words were written continuously, as in the ancient Greek manuscripts, but the discovery of the ancient
writing on the Moabite stone indicates that this was not so.
The words on the Moabite stone are separated by points,
and the text is separated into parts or verses by vertical
strokes. There are about 7000 words in the old Hebrew
vocabulary.

18. *The Massorah* is a collection of critical and other notes
relating to the Hebrew text of the Old Testament. These
were intended to preserve the text in a certain fixed character. The notes of the Massorites referred to—(1) What is in
the text? (2) What should be in the text? They counted
the letters; they marked the *wauv* in Lev. 11 : 42 as the
middle letter in the Pentateuch. They noted that the letter *aleph* (A) occurs 42,377 times, and *beth* (B) 35,288
times, and so on of each letter in the Hebrew alphabet.
They noted when a word occurred only once, and a multitude of other minute points about the text.

But in making a new copy, they sometimes found a word in the written copy before them, which they had reason to believe was incorrect.   They would not alter it, but they would write in the margin the consonants of the word they believed to be the right one.   Then they would add under the word in the text the vowel points of the right word which they had written in the margin.   The word in the text they called *Kethibh*—" What is written ; " the word in the margin *Keri*—" What must be read."   The ancient Hebrew was written without vowels.   The vowel points were the invention of the Massorites between 500 and 1000 A.D. to represent and stereotype, as it were, the traditional reading of the text which had come down to their time. Hebrew can be read, though with greater difficulty, without vowel points, or accents.

CHAPTER VI.

THE NEW TESTAMENT : HOW AND WHEN ONE BOOK.

1. THE BOOK A GROWTH.—The New Testament was a growth. The gathering of the separate books into one volume was a gradual process. The books to be excluded and those to be included in the collection were not selected by the decree of any church council, nor decided by an apostle or apostolic men ; nor was the collection the result of any single inspired act of a Christian Father or scholar, nor of a local body of believers, like the church at Antioch, Jerusalem or Rome.

2. *The Result of a General Agreement.*—The collection of the various writings into one book, now called the New Testament, was the result of a general agreement among all early Christians scattered over the then known civilized world. The line between those writings which were regarded "sacred" and of divine authority, and those that were "apocryphal," was sharply drawn in the fourth century. The persecution of Christians under Diocletian (A.D. 303) was directed against their sacred books as well as against their faith and person. The order was to burn all copies of their Scriptures, and Christians were forced to give them up or be condemned themselves. Some gave up their Scriptures,and were branded as *traditores* (traitors) by their fellow-disciples. Others *apparently* complied by giving up heretical or apocryphal writings, and thus escaped

the censure of the church. This required a definite agreement among Christians respecting what were and what were not Scriptures of divine authority.

3. *A Testing Process.*—Such an agreement was not reached at once, nor without severely testing a few of the writings finally admitted, as Hebrews in the western church, and seven books (James, Jude, 2 Peter, 2 and 3 John, Hebrews and Revelation) by some in the eastern church. But by the end of the fourth century objections and doubts respecting those books were silenced. The Latin church of the north also concurred in the same list of sacred books, and the collection as we now have it was universally regarded as closed.[1]

4. *The Tests.*—This collection remained "closed" until the Reformation, in the sixteenth century, when Luther and some of the reformers revived doubts in respect to the *antilegomena* books, because of the doctrines they were supposed to teach. Yet Protestant Christians have with great unanimity accepted the strict collection of sacred books as it was accepted and "closed" by the early Christian church in the third and fourth centuries.

The crucial tests which a book must pass before it could be accepted as of divine authority do not come within the scope of these papers. The purpose here is to state, historically, what writings were accepted. It may be proper, however, to add that Protestants require more than the external testimony of the church to certify what writings are sacred and of divine authority. Thus Luther against Eck said, "A council cannot make that to be of Scripture

---

[1] See Weiss, Intro., vol. i. p. 119 ff.; Schaff, *Hist. Christn. Church*, vol. iii. p. 608 ff.; Eusebius, *H. E.*, bk. iii. 25, bk. vi. 25.

which is not by nature Scripture." Calvin called it "a most pernicious error" to hold "that the Scriptures have only so much weight as is conceded to them by the suffrages of the church; as though," he adds, "the eternal and inviolable truth of God depended on the arbitrary will of men." (Inst. 1 : 7.) The Helvetic, Gallican, Anglican, Scotch and Westminster Confessions uniformly maintain this principle respecting the Scriptures. The test of a book to a place in the Scriptures may be stated as threefold : (1) external evidence, as the historic testimony of the church; (2) internal evidence from the book itself, determined in part by the consensus of Christian scholarship; and (3) witness of the Spirit to the truth and authority of the word in the heart of believers. See 2d Helvetic Conf., chaps. i., ii. ; Gallican Conf., art. iv. ; Belgian, art. v. ; Thirty-nine Articles, art. vi. ; Scotch Conf., 1560, art. xix. ; Westminster Conf., art. i., § 2-5 ; Reuss, *Hist. Canon*, 313.

5. *Fresh Examination.*—Biblical study is taken up afresh with each new generation of scholars; and the object is to search for the external and internal evidence concerning each New Testament book. The decision depends in part upon the test of admission to the collection. The tendency is to make this test apply not alone to what is apostolic, but to include what belongs to apostolic times and was attested by the general religious consciousness of early Christians.

6. *Formation in the Western Church.*—In marking the process of gathering apostolic writings into one New Testament, let it be noticed that councils and the great Christian Fathers did not decide nor so strongly discuss what writings *ought* to be included, as *declare what in fact were accepted* and included among those of divine authority. It

appears, however, that generally, early Christians devoutly applied substantially the same principles to test the nature of each book of the New Testament as later Protestant Christians have applied. The early Christians further required that the books must be written by an apostle or apostolic men, and must have been adopted for reading in public service.

In the western church all the writings now in the New Testament were readily acknowledged, except Hebrews. The hesitation in respect to Hebrews sprang largely from the uncertainty as to the author. Some held that it was written by Paul, but many doubted its Pauline authorship. The frequent contact of western with eastern Christians, however, and the studies of Origen, Ambrose, Augustine, Rufinus and Jerome, led to the general acceptance of the Epistle to the Hebrews in the western church about the close of the fourth century, and the New Testament collection was "closed" as we now have it. The West had no desire to include other writings beyond these in the Scriptures. See Weiss, Intro., vol. i. p. 137.

7. *Formation in the Eastern Church.*—It was a more difficult process to perfect the collection of New Testament writings in the East. At a very early period at least twenty books were admitted without question. These were sometimes called *homolegomena*, that is, "acknowledged." The remaining seven books were referred to as *antilegomena*, that is, "objected to," meaning that some were uncertain whether they had a right to a place in the collection or not.

Eusebius wrote a history of the church in the fourth century. In his narrative of the first and second centuries he gives a statement of the books of the New Testament.

He asserts that twenty books were acknowledged without question. Some hesitated to accept Revelation, "but others rank it among the genuine." Among other *antilegomena*, or books that were questioned, although he says "they are well known and approved by many," he mentions James, Jude, 2 Peter, 2 and 3 John—in all five. He then refers to several books as spurious—as the Acts of Paul, Shepherd of Hermas, Epistle of Barnabas, Revelation of Peter, and Institutions of the Apostles. When Eusebius comes to the period of Origen, he quotes the testimony of that Father, that the Revelation of John and the Epistle to the Hebrews were then accepted, but reports that some still have doubts respecting 2 Peter and 2 and 3. John, although he implies that the many receive them as genuine portions of Scripture. *H. E.* vi. 25.

8. EARLY CATALOGUE OF NEW TESTAMENT BOOKS.—In the writings that have been preserved of the early Christian Fathers of the first four centuries, not less than eight or ten catalogues, more or less complete, of the books of the New Testament are given, and scores of writers quote from the New Testament books as of divine authority.[1] When it is considered how very small a portion of those early writings has come down to us, this evidence will be counted of great value. Augustine gives a full list corresponding to those now accepted, as do Athanasius, Jerome and Eusebius. Some of these omit Revelation, and some Hebrews also. In all the Christian writings of importance belonging to that early period that have come down to us, the books of the New Testament are referred to, quoted or accepted as sacred and of divine authority. The citations

---

[1] See Lardner's works.

by some of these early writers, as Justin Martyr of the second century, and Origen, would fill a volume. These references and quotations are widely distributed, including writers of each century, from those of Clemens Romanus and Ignatius of the first century to those of Augustine, Chrysostom and Cyril of Alexandria, near the close of the fourth century.

9. *Process of Forming the Collection.*—The beginning and the steps in the process of gathering the sacred writings into one book of divine authority rest in some obscurity. Yet the main features are indicated in the fragmentary works of contemporary writers, and accord with similar known facts of history.

While the apostles were proclaiming the gospel, Christians looked to them for authoritative instruction, and did not feel the need of written teachings upon matters of faith and belief. Yet Paul wrote brief instructions to the churches he had planted at Thessalonica and in Galatia, which are now generally acknowledged to be the earliest written books in the form found in the New Testament, and date from about the middle of the first century.[1] Most of the books have internal evidence that they were written before the fall of Jerusalem, A.D. 70; that all of them date before the end of the first century has been successfully proven. Some critical scholars of the destructive school

---

[1] Papias, of Hierapolis, in the early part of the second century, speaks of βιβλια—books from which the commands of the Lord might be known—and alludes to a history written by Mark, and a collection of "sayings" in Hebrew made by Matthew. Even the epistles of Barnabas and of Clement clearly have statements in almost the exact words of Matthew. The second epistle of Clement and the *Didache* have clear evidence of the influence of Luke's Gospel. Compare Weiss, Intro., i. 38, 39.

who have sought to maintain a later date have been forced to abandon their position and concede a date not far from the close of the first century.

As the number of Christians increased, and became too numerous for the apostles and their immediate disciples to instruct orally, there was a necessity for writings of authority to preserve the church in purity and prevent serious heresies and unbelief. In fact, history tells us that divisions and heretical views did prevail in many quarters, and even that spurious works were written and circulated under the cover of apostolic names. The true believers, therefore, gathered the genuine writings of the apostolic age, and the New Testament collection began to be formed. In the second century, Christian writers, as Dionysius of Corinth and Theophilus of Antioch (A.D. 180), refer to the "Scriptures of the Lord" as of the same authority as the Old Testament. The testimony of history is clear that twenty books, comprising eight-ninths of the entire New Testament, were thus generally accepted as Holy Scripture by the early Christians from 170 A.D. and onward.

10. *Completion of the New Testament.*—Although the other seven books already mentioned were more slow in securing universal acknowledgment, yet they were finally so accepted, while others, as the Epistle of Barnabas and the Shepherd of Hermas, were rejected. The sharp persecutions which the early Christians endured, called for a most careful and devout spiritual testing of every writing; for the acceptance of a work as "sacred" and of divine authority might put their lives in jeopardy. It was only natural that some should hesitate to accept a few books, perhaps less known from their small size or the peculiar character of their contents than were the other books. It

is not inconsistent with this natural process of gathering the
books of the New Testament to hold, as some do, that the
Gospels and Acts were early formed into one collection, to
which the apostolic teachings were added. Nor is it improbable that these apostolic epistles were circulated by
themselves for a brief period. But that they were finally
accepted in the face of such circumstances is strong proof
of their title to a place in the New Testament. The
Council of Carthage (397 A.D.) declared that "besides the
canonical Scriptures, nothing [is to] be read in the church
under the title of divine Scriptures." It then adds a list
of the books accepted as canonical, which besides the Old
Testament includes the twenty-seven New Testament books
and no others.

In this gradual process of sifting out of the mass of writings of the apostolic period, and of testing and settling which
were of divine authority, we find that while several books
were on the line of doubt and some were rejected, only
seven of the New Testament books were ever on that line,
and that these stood the test and were finally admitted.
The chief hesitation was over five of these books, comprising only about one-thirty-sixth part of the entire New
Testament.

11. *Attested by the Church and the Spirit.*—The conclusion is that the great body of early Christians, the general
church of Jesus Christ, of every speech, East and West,
Syrian, Asiatic, African and European, devoutly seeking
to know the mind of Christ, was led by the Spirit of God
to fix upon these twenty-seven books and no others as the
New Testament Scriptures having divine authority as the
word of God. This is far more satisfactory, and gives us
a much stronger attestation and assurance of the purity

and authority of this collection as the word of God, than if
it had been made and decreed by a church council, or only
by the early Christian Fathers, as Augustine, Jerome, Tertullian, Origen, Irenæus, Cyril, Justin Martyr or Polycarp.
They testify that the church universal, guided by the Spirit,
did receive these books as the word of God; and thus the
promise of Christ to the apostles was fulfilled: " When he,
the Spirit of truth, is come, he shall guide you into all the
truth " (John 16: 13, Revised Version).

CHAPTER VII.

WRITERS AND COMPOSITION OF THE NEW TESTAMENT BOOKS.

1. *Variety in Writing.*—All the books now in the New Testament were extant and widely accepted as of divine authority within one hundred years of the apostolic era. The collection was "closed" and universally accepted as "Holy Scriptures," of equal rank and authority with the Old Testament, within two centuries after the apostolic founding of Christian churches.

The twenty-seven New Testament books were written by eight or nine different writers. They had widely different temperaments, traits of character and physical circumstances, and had, moreover, widely different modes and degrees of educational training.

Paul was the finished Jewish university student, a master of logic and of argument. Luke was the Greek medical scholar; Matthew the orderly, practical man of business, conversing with equal ease and grace in Aramaic and Greek; while John was the well-to-do fisherman, earnest, meditative, the man to make a profound Christian philosopher when the opportunity came.

More definitely then, the questions before us are : When, by whom, under what circumstances, and with what purpose, were the twenty-seven books of the New Testament originally written ?

2. *Date of the Books.*—The thirteen Pauline Epistles

(excepting those to individuals) were among the earliest of the present written books of the New Testament. They may all be safely placed within a limit of fifteen years, from A.D. 52 to A.D. 67.

The date of the Synoptic Gospels and of the Acts may with much confidence be placed within the ten years from A.D. 60 to A.D. 70. Within the same period may be safely placed the pastoral Epistles of Paul, the Epistle to the Hebrews, and the general Epistles of James, Peter, and Jude.

The Gospel of John, his three Epistles and Revelation, belong to the last quarter of the first century, the Gospel probably written earliest, the epistles next, and the Revelation last, from 90 to 95; but the Gospel probably published last, 95 to 100 A.D.

3. *Writers of the Books.*—The names of eight of the writers of twenty-six of the New Testament books are certainly known. Six of the writers thus named have been identified beyond reasonable question. Concerning two of them, James and Jude, it is not yet agreed which of the several persons called James, nor which of those called Jude or Judas, is the author of the respective epistles bearing these names.

In eighteen of the New Testament books the writers distinctly state their names in the body of their respective books. In nine of the books the name of the writer is not given in the works themselves. The authors of the nine must be ascertained, if at all, from other sources, such as the historic testimony of the early Christians immediately following the apostolic period, and the internal evidences found in the books themselves. For example, the book may contain hints pointing to the identity of the writer, such as are given in John 21: 24; with 20: 31; 13: 23, and in the " we " sections of Acts 21 : 1 ; 27 : 1, compared with Acts 1 : 1 and Luke 1 : 3. The structure, style and topics of a book, by agreeing with what is known of the character and circumstances of the person whom history indicates as the writer, may confirm the authorship.

4. THE GOSPELS AND THE ACTS do not give the names of their respective authors. Historical testimony from the first half of the second century declares that the first Gospel was written by Matthew, one of the twelve, and who was first called Levi. Papias (A.D. 130–160) says, "Matthew composed his history [of our Lord] in the Hebrew dialect, and everyone translated it as he was able."[1] Irenæus makes a similar statement, adding that the Gospel was written while the apostles were preaching in Rome.

5. But the Gospel of Matthew, as we now have it, reads like a Greek original. Certain passages in which it agrees with Mark and Luke indicate that the writer used a Greek source. How can it be that the Gospel was written in Hebrew, and yet our Greek copy not be a translation? An answer is not difficult. Matthew, as a tax collector, would become familiar with Aramaic and Greek. For Hebrews, he would naturally have first written his Gospel in Aramaic. Then the Hellenistic Christians would desire it in Greek, and he wrote it in Greek also for them. The Hebrew copy has perished, and the Greek alone has been preserved. There is a similar parallel in the writings of Josephus in the same era. His history of the Jewish wars was first written in Aramaic, but afterwards in Greek. The Aramaic copy has perished; the one in Greek has been preserved to our time.

---

[1] Eusebius, H. E. 3 : 39.

5

6. Historic testimony has uniformly fixed upon Mark as the author of the second Gospel.[1]   Nor is there any reasonable doubt that he is the same as John Mark,[2] the son of Mary, at whose house Peter found the disciples praying in Jerusalem (Acts 12 : 12).   His Gospel is frequently quoted by Justin Martyr and Irenæus.   The latter says, "Mark, the disciple and interpreter of Peter, himself also wrote and handed on to us what Peter had preached."

7. That the third Gospel and the Acts were written by the same hand is fairly proven by the opening sentences of the books themselves (compare Luke 1 : 3 with Acts 1 : 1), and by the construction and style of the two treatises.   That Luke the physician and companion of Paul is the writer, history testifies, and the circumstantial evidence derived from the books and what we know of Luke confirm that testimony.

8. *The Fourth Gospel.*—The authorship of the fourth Gospel was for years the chief object of attack by skeptical critics.   If they could prove that to be not genuine, or not trustworthy, they could then hope to destroy the other historic foundations of Christianity.   They signally failed. That the apostle John was the writer of that Gospel has been established against the severest and strongest critical objections.

The authenticity of the Gospel has been established by the fact of the general acceptance of it in the last part of the second century, by citations from it as Apostolic

---

[1] Papias states what John the Presbyter said, " Mark being the interpreter of Peter, whatsoever he recorded he wrote with great accuracy," etc. (Eusebius, II. E. 3 : 39).

[2] "Without doubt he is identical with John Mark " (Weiss, *Intro.*, 2 : 256).

Memoirs of Christ by Justin Martyr, by its use among various Gnostic sects, and by evidence attached to the book itself. See John 21 : 24, 25.[1] In the face of this irrefragable evidence, the efforts to deny that John wrote the fourth Gospel, because a plain fisherman could not be fitted to write such a book, or could not be the author of the book of Revelation and of so dissimilar a work as the Gospel, are shallow reasonings, or mere "begging the question" under color of specious argument. Few would believe *a priori* that a poor tinker like Bunyan could have written the most famous uninspired book in the world, the *Pilgrim's Progress;* yet no sane person doubts that Bunyan did write it. And who can doubt that the apostle John, taught three years by a divine Teacher, followed by a long life of study, observation and experience in Christian truth, and guided by the Holy Spirit, could write the Gospel ascribed to him, and that he would also possess versatility enough to write a work as different from the Gospel as Revelation? Literary writers on secular topics and of far less training and experience show as wide a versatility. It is unscientific and puerile to urge that a Christian writer with the advantages and experience history assures us that John possessed, and with the added power of the Holy Spirit, was without equal versatility. The writer of that Gospel was a Palestinian Jew, an eye-witness of the events he narrates, and the book claims to be by the disciple whom Jesus loved. These particulars apply best to the apostle John and to him alone.

---

[1] These verses are commonly held by critical scholars to have been added to the Gospel by the elders of the church over which John was pastor, and who provided the first copy of his Gospel for transcription. See Abbot, *Authorship of the Fourth Gospel,* p. 90.

9. *Pauline Epistles.*—In each of the THIRTEEN EPIS-TLES of Paul, the writer distinctly avows himself to be the apostle of that name. If they were not by him, then they are bold forgeries. Who believes that treatises of this kind that were deliberate forgeries would have held or gained the confidence of the church universal, and during the life-time of many intimate pupils of that great apostle? None, except the critics of the destructive school of Bauer and of Renan, doubt that these epistles were all written by Paul. Even they are compelled to admit most of them to be genuine. The historic evidence is clear that they were the writings of Paul.

10. *The Hebrews.*—The writer of the *book of Hebrews* is unknown, or at least undetermined. The authorship was an open question as long ago as the days of Origen. In the early eastern church the belief was that Paul wrote it, or that it was his treatise although it might have been penned by Luke or Clement. But in the early western church the author was believed to be Barnabas or some unknown writer. In later times Luther advocated Apollos as the author, while Erasmus urged Clement.

11. *James.*—The *Epistle of James* could not have been written by James, son of Zebedee and the brother of John, for it was written after the persecution, and hence after James was slain by Herod. The writer was a James whose pastoral authority he assumed would not be questioned by the Jewish Christians "scattered abroad." This fits well with what history tells us of James the "bishop" of Jerusalem. Whether he was identical with James the son of Alphæus (which is doubtful) or James the brother of the Lord, or was another James, cannot be discussed here for want of space. It must suffice to say that it is not incon-

sistent with the main historic facts to regard James the writer of this Epistle as identical with the "bishop" of Jerusalem and with James the brother of the Lord.

12. *Peter.*—THE TWO EPISTLES OF PETER are clearly ascribed to Simon Peter, one of the twelve. The first Epistle was universally accepted by the early Church as the work of Peter, which the style and contents strongly confirm. The author aims to comfort Christians who were suffering for their religion. They were the Christian Jews scattered through the Roman provinces of Asia Minor. The second Epistle claims to be by Peter and to be the "second" which he had written (2 Pet. 3 : 1). It was held among the doubtful books for some time, but, after a careful sifting of the evidences for its Petrine authorship, it was accepted as genuine. The resemblances of style between this and the first Epistle are greater than the differences, and these differences spring chiefly from the different purpose and persons for which the two books were written. Hope is the keynote of the first, since those addressed were persecuted for their faith. Knowledge is emphasized in the second, since it was written to those exposed to false teaching, but, in fact, holiness is the *theme* of both Epistles.

13. *John's Epistles.*—THE FIRST EPISTLE OF JOHN was generally received by the early Church as written by John the beloved disciple and one of the twelve. In contents and style it agrees well with the fourth Gospel. It was intended to guard against false teachings and to confirm the faith of believers in Jesus as the Son of God. It was first written for the church at Ephesus and for Christians in that region. The two smaller epistles of John were widely, though not universally, received as the letters of John in

the time of Origen, and, after long testing, were finally received as genuine.   The second is addressed to "the elect
lady and her children," which probably refers to some
church in a house, similar to that in the house of Aquila
and Priscilla (1 Cor. 16 : 19 ; Rom. 16 : 3, 5).   The third
Epistle of John was written to Gaius, perhaps one of those
elsewhere named (Rom. 16 : 23 ; 1 Cor. 1 : 14; Acts 19 :
29; 20: 4).   It describes the state of the Church near the
close of the first century.   The date of all John's epistles
must be placed late in the first century, though possibly a
little earlier than that of Revelation.

14. *Jude.*—THE SHORT EPISTLE OF JUDE is recognized
by writers who are silent respecting that of James.   Precisely which Jude it was who was "the brother of James"
depends upon which James is intended.   If Jude had been
an apostle, he would naturally have been expected to write
as an apostle.   That he should designate himself as "the
brother of James" is incidental proof that he was not the
apostle Jude.   He cites some apocryphal books,[1] but so Paul
also cites from heathen poets.   His Epistle reminds one of
the second Epistle of Peter.   These striking resemblances
have not been very satisfactorily explained.   Formerly it
was suggested that the two writers used a common docu-
ment, but later critics regard the likenesses either as mere
coincidences, or that possibly the letter of Peter may have
unconsciously influenced the language and expression of
Jude.   The letter was apparently written for Palestinian
Jews, about 67 to 70 A.D.

15. *The Book of Revelation* is a product of a period of
trial and of hope.   Clearly it is largely prophetic, and it is

---

[1] *Book of Enoch*, and, according to Origen, *Assumption of Moses.*

now generally conceded that it was written by the apostle John. The integrity and unity of the book have been sharply attacked by modern critics, but their arguments have been shown to be weak and their view untenable. The interpretation of the book is confessedly hedged about with the most serious difficulties. It is the favorite field for the mystic, the fanciful and the imaginative biblical expositors.

• There is little doubt that it was first written to warn Christians of coming persecutions and to comfort them in their terrible sufferings. It points the martyrs to the reward beyond this life and to the peace and glories of the celestial home.

TABLE OF NEW TESTAMENT BOOKS.

By whom, to whom, when and where written, and the subject of each book.

N. B.—The dates are approximate only. The place of writing is also not certain. The titles of the books and the statement at the end of the Epistles in our English version are not by the original writer, but were added by some subsequent hand.

Book.	Writer.	Where Written.	Date.	To Whom.	Topic.
Matt.....	Matthew...........	Judæa.. ...	60–64	Jewish Chris'ns.	Jesus the Messiah.
Mark.. .	Mark...	Rome (?)..	60–67	Roman Chris'ns.	Jesus the Son of Man.
Luke......	Luke...............	Cæsarea or Rome (?).	58–65	Theophilus	Jesus the World's Redeemer.
John.....	John	Ephesus or Patmos [1]	90–98 [1] ...	All Christians	Jesus the Eternal Son of God.
Acts.....	Luke...............	Rome	65, 66 ...	Theophilus.........	Planting of Apostolic Churches.
Rom.....	Paul................	Corinth	58	Roman Chris'ns.	Sin and Grace.
1 Cor....	"	Ephesus ...	57	Ch. at Corinth...	Unity and Resurrection in Christ.
2 Cor....	"	Macedonia	57	" " ...	Christian Graces.
Gal.......	"	Ephesus ...	56, 57	Ch. at Galatia....	Salvation by Faith.
Eph......	"	Rome........	61–63.. .	Ch. at Ephesus...	Principles, Life and Unity of the Church.
Phil......	"	"	61–63.....	Ch. at Philippi...	Personal Counsels.
Col.......	"	"	61–63	Ch. at Colosse.....	Correcting False Doctrines.
1 Thess.	"	Corinth....	52.........	Ch. at Thessal'a.	Holiness and Second Coming.

[1] Whether the last chapter is an appendix or not, it is quite clear that 21 : 24, 25 was added, probably by the Church at Ephesus, before the publication of the Gospel. Thus it may have been written while John was first at Ephesus, but not circulated until his exile in Patmos.

TABLE OF NEW TESTAMENT BOOKS—*Continued*.

Book.	Writers.	Where Written.	Date.	To Whom.	Topic.
2 Thess.	Paul................	Corinth	52, 53	Ch. at Thessal'a.	Correcting Wrong Views of First Letter.
1 Tim...	"	Macedonia	57 or 65[1]	Timothy............	Duties of Church Officers.
2 Tim...	"	Rome.......	64 or 67[1]	"	Triumphant Faith.
Titus....	"	Macedonia	65...........	Titus	Special Rules for the Pastor.
Philem..	"	Rome......	61–63....	Philemon	Freedom and Slavery.
Heb......	Paul, Barnabas or Apollos (?) [2]	Italy (?)....	63–66.....	Judæan Chris'ns	Christ's Priesthood Superior to the Mosaic.
James...	James, brother of the Lord (?)	Jerusalem.	62–63	" "	Works, Faith and Prayer.
1 Peter..	Simon Peter......	Babylon...	64...	Scattered Jewish Christians.	Duties of Christians to One Another.
2 Peter..	" "		66(?)	To all Christians	A New Heaven and Earth.
1 John..	Apostle John.....	Ephesus...	90–95	Believers............	Redeeming Love.
2 John..	" "	" ...	"	Elect Lady.........	Obedience to Christ.
3 John..	" "	" ...	"	Gaius................	Personal Piety.
Jude.....	Jude................	Jerusalem.	65–90.....	Jewish Chris'ns.	Against Dangerous Doctrines.
Rev... ...	Apostle John.....	Patmos (?)	95–100...	Seven ch's, Asia.	The Church in Conflict and Glory.

[1] The date depends upon whether there was a second imprisonment of Paul at Rome. If there was, the latter date is the correct one.

[2] Opinions of critical scholars are now divided between the three, with the tendency not very strong against the Pauline authorship of Hebrews.

CHAPTER VIII.

THE OLD TESTAMENT: HOW AND WHEN ONE BOOK.

The several books composing the Old Testament were written at different times, stretching over a period of about one thousand years. They span the ten centuries from Moses and the exodus to the return from the Babylonian captivity and the era of Ezra and Malachi. Like the building of a vast, magnificent palace, the production and gathering into one book of all these varied writings of the law, the prophets and the psalms, was a slow process.

1. *Books in Septuagint Bible.*—In the first centuries of the Christian era the Septuagint or Greek version of the Hebrew Scriptures was in common use. Along with this version of the generally-accepted books of the Hebrew Bible, certain other apocryphal works were placed for reference, and thus came into favor and were not infrequently quoted as if those works possessed the authority of the sacred books themselves. But the sharp controversies of the Jews with their opponents caused them to point out precisely the real difference between the Greek collection and their Hebrew Bible, and to define more clearly the books which were accepted as of divine authority—that is, the books really comprised in the Hebrew Old Testament.

2. *Testimony of Origen and Josephus.*—The early Christians also saw the necessity of fixing upon a list in accord with the historic belief of the Hebrews. Thus Origen

(81)

(186–254 A.D.) made a list of these Old Testament books, based upon the historic views prevailing among the Jews. Josephus recognized a *definite and distinct body of books* as sacred. The efforts recently made to belittle the testimony of Josephus on this point indicate greater ingenuity than candor. It is said that he does not furnish an "authentic list." But from his definite statement it is certain there was a body of sacred books well known and generally accepted; and from other historic sources the books in the main can be satisfactorily determined. His words are worth citing: "We have not an innumerable multitude of books among us, disagreeing and contradicting one another [as the Greeks have], but only twenty-two books, which contain the records of all the past times; which are justly believed to be divine." He then describes them as five books of Moses, thirteen written by the prophets, and four books of poems and "precepts for the conduct of human life." *Contra Apion*, 1 : 8. By a common usage of the Jews, the books were counted twenty-two (but more frequently twenty-four), to correspond with the letters in the Hebrew alphabet. As the two books of Samuel were reckoned one, and the two of Kings one, and the two of Chronicles one, and Lamentations was a part of Jeremiah, and the twelve minor prophets were counted one only, the collection noted by Josephus is substantially that now accepted. It is conceded by Eichhorn and others that Josephus quotes all the books of the Talmudic canon except four; but two of these must be counted in his four books of poetry, to wit, Proverbs and Ecclesiastes. This leaves only the Song of Solomon and possibly Job uncertain in his list.

3. *The Triple Division.*—Professor Strack, a foremost

Hebraist, holds the statement of Josephus to be of the "strongest testimony for the canon, and, as is evident, expresses the national and not his private views." He further urges that, in the twenty-two books, Josephus counted Job and the Song of Solomon. Moreover Strack declares that the triple division of the books in the Hebrew Old Testament is affirmed in the prologue to Sirach, and in the New Testament, Luke 24: 44.[1]

4. *What Philo and Talmudists say.*—The Talmudists, however, commonly reckoned the number of the Old Testament books twenty-four. This could easily be made by separating some of the books counted as one in the Jewish schools of Alexandria. Philo quotes as of divine authority thirty of the thirty-nine books; so that, passing by the disputed passage in his writings mentioning the books that were in the Old Testament, he quotes all the books that we would expect, from his topic and style, that he would cite, except possibly two books.

5. *What Christ and New Testament Writers Say.*—To this must be added the direct if not conclusive testimony of the New Testament. In the apostolic writings it is clear that groups of works, and a body of books regarded as a unit, are repeatedly alluded to as of divine authority. What those separate writings were may and can be ascertained by evidence sufficient to satisfy a candid and an impartial mind. The Hebrew Scriptures are frequently referred to, or quoted under groups of books, as "the law," "the law of Moses," or simply "Moses," "the prophets," and the psalms, or sometimes "the writings," that is, "the

---

[1] Professor Briggs (*Biblical Study*, p. 131) objects to this, but his objection is inconclusive.

Scriptures" in the narrow sense. They are alluded to as a unit, one divine record; "the Scriptures" in the broader sense.[1]

Christ quoted the Jewish "Scriptures" as sacred books of divine authority. By "Scriptures" he did not refer simply to the K'tubim or Hagiographa, that is, the so-called third group; for the passages thus cited were frequently from the prophets, which belonged to the so-called second group. For example, "not knowing the Scriptures," Matt. 22: 29, 31, evidently has reference to Ex. 3: 6; and "how then shall the Scriptures be fulfilled?" refers to Isa. 53: 10; and a similar phrase in Mark 15: 28 is followed by a citation from Isa. 53: 12.

6. OLD TESTAMENT BOOKS QUOTED IN THE NEW.—Not less than thirty of the thirty-nine Old Testament books are quoted in the New Testament. Our Lord Himself quotes from twenty of them. There are about 280 direct quotations (including those in Revelation) of passages and clauses, and about 220 references to incidents and indirect quotations in the New Testament (exclusive of Revelation)[2] from the Old Testament. The book of Revelation

---

[1] For notice of the Old Testament books in the commonly-accepted groups, see Matt. 5: 17; 7: 12; 12: 5; 22: 40; Mark 1: 2; John 1: 45; 7: 19; 8: 5; 15: 25; Luke 10: 26; 24: 44. For reference to them as one work, see Matt. 21: 42; 22: 29; 26: 54; Mark 12: 24; 14: 49; Luke 24: 27, 32, 45; John 5: 39; Acts 17: 2, 11; 18: 24; Rom. 1: 2; 15: 4; 16: 26; 1 Cor. 15: 3; 2 Tim. 3: 15; 2 Pet. 3: 16. Those who assert that when Jesus referred to the group called the Psalms, which included all the books not in the groups of the law and of the prophets, he referred only to the single book of Psalms and not to the group so called, are simply "begging the whole question" at issue.

[2] Some older writers roughly counted 265 direct quotations and 350 allusions in the New Testament from the Old. The latest tables in Bagster's new "Helps to Bible Study" note about 850 such direct

is almost a mosaic of thoughts, figures and expressions, from the prophetic books of the Old Testament.[1]

Again, the numerous citations in the Gospels and Epistles clearly indicate that some divisions in the Hebrew Scriptures were recognized and well known in that era, while at the same time all these groups were known as one work, called, by way of eminence, "the Scriptures."

7. *The Synod of Jamnia.*—It is generally agreed that the books rightfully having a place in the Jewish Scriptures were definitely fixed by the assembly or council at Jamnia, in the time of the Jewish war with Titus about A.D. 70. There was a dissenting minority among the Essenes and Zealots, who would include apocryphal books, and doubtless some among Sadducees and Samaritans, all of whom held views of doctrines more or less heretical. But the majority of the assembly agreed upon the generally accepted books held to be of divine authority.

Some of the Grecian Jews of Alexandria were broad in their views, favoring the apocryphal books, and had placed them in their Greek version of the Old Testament; but there was no Alexandrian canon.[2] The Sadducees would naturally reject any book that favored future life and a resurrection, doctrines which they denied; while the Sa-

and indirect quotations and allusions. The tables in Oxford "Helps to the Study of the Bible" give a good list of exact quotations and a somewhat less complete list of indirect quotations and allusions.

[1] From a careful examination of the book of Revelation, it appears that in fifteen passages the book of Revelation uses the exact language and expressions of some Old Testament book, besides 129 distinct allusions to the Old Testament, and upwards of 100 less distinct references. Bagster's "Helps" note only six citations, aside from "allusions" in Revelation to the Old Testament.

[2] The old Syrian Church did not accept the Old Testament Apocrypha. The books are not in the Peshito version, though found in later Syrian versions.

maritan party was loth to accept any except the five books
of Moses as of divine authority. Yet the ablest Biblical
scholars maintain that the Jews of Egypt held that the
same books belonged to the Old Testament, as did the
Jews of Palestine.[1]

8. How Formed.—It is natural to suppose that special
veneration of sacred books written by authors of promi-
nence would first appear, and that too when the power of
the revealing spirit had been exceptionally clear and strong.
This would begin with the books of Moses and those associated with them, and then extend to the more earnest and
spiritual of the prophets.[2] How much earlier than the
Council of Jamnia the entire collection of Old Testament
books was completed and fixed it is not possible definitely
to state. The statement of Josephus implies a date some
centuries before the Christian era. He says, after the passage quoted above, "How firmly we have given credit to
these books of our own nation is evident by what we do;
for during so many ages as have already passed, no one has
been so bold as either to add anything to them, to take
anything from them, or to make any change in them; but
it is become natural to all Jews. . . . to esteem these books
to contain divine doctrines, to persist in them, and if oc-
casion be, willingly to die for them." *Contra Apion*, 1 : 8.

Josephus here advocates the Hebrew Scriptures as
against Greeks, and appears to point to the persecution
against the sacred books of the Jews which followed the
Maccabæan wars about 160 B. C. It seems fair to infer,
therefore, that the Hebrew Scriptures, accepted in Jose-

---

[1] So Eichhorn, De Wette, Keil and Hävernick. Bleek and some
others dissent.
[2] So Dr. Dillmann argues.

phus' day were completed and accepted at the period of
this persecution. The Son of Sirach, in a prologue to
Ecclesiasticus, strengthens this view by his testimony.

9. *Ezra and the Great Synagogue.*—There is, indeed, an
oral tradition, reduced to writing at a later period, that the
collection of Old Testament books was made under divine
appointment by Ezra, or by the hundred and twenty men
of the Great Synagogue ; but this tradition, though widely
prevalent among the Jews for centuries, has not been traced
to any satisfactory historical sources, and is stoutly disputed by modern critical scholars. Whether the collection
of Old Testament books was or was not made by the Great
Synagogue, or by Ezra, Nehemiah or Malachi, or some of
the last of the prophets, it is certain that there was such a
complete collection for two or three centuries, at least, before the Christian era, and that there was a book of the
law, the germ of the collection of divine authority, known
eight or ten centuries earlier. See 2 Chron. 34: 15 ; Josh.
1 : 8 ; 8 : 34 ; Deut. 30 : 10 ; 31 : 26.

10. *Slow Growth.*—The New Testament was the product
and result of a single century ; the Old Testament the
growth of ten centuries, and of great eras in the Hebrew
national life. It was certainly complete and well defined in
the period of persecution of Antiochus (168 B. C.) In
that period the sacred books were sought out and burnt, and
possession of a " book of the covenant " was punished by
death.

11. *Objections Answered.*—The dissent from the strict
Jewish list of Old Testament books is only partial and apparent, not real or partaking of any national character.
The unsettled state of the Hebrew people after the exile,
their persecutions and distracting wars, and the various

heresies that sprang from interchanging with Gentile peoples, account for the "controversies" respecting their religion and sacred books. There was no serious questioning of the divine authority of the books; nor are the few references to the apocryphal books any conclusive proof that they were regarded as Scriptures. Philo never uses the apocryphal in the same way that he does the canonical books. Josephus expressly disclaims divine authority for the apocryphal writings.[1]

It is safe, therefore, to conclude, from historical and other evidence, that the books of the Old Testament were gathered into one and accepted as of divine authority by the general consensus of godly Jewish people, and that the collection was completed from two to three centuries before the Christian era. This collection has been generally accepted as the entire books belonging to the Old Testament by the early Syrian Church and by all bodies of modern evangelical and Protestant churches. The Latin Church accepted the same also, with the addition of some apocryphal books.

12. *Order of the Books.*—The order of the Old Testament books in the Hebrew Bible is not the same as in our common English Bibles. In the face of the rigid rules for making copies of the Hebrew Scriptures, the variations found in Hebrew manuscripts and in Hebrew printed Bibles number about thirty thousand (some estimate two hundred thousand), but they are mostly quite unimportant. The Old Testament we have now is substantially that of

---

[1] " It is true, our history hath been written since Artaxerxes very particularly, but it hath not been esteemed of the like authority with the former by our forefathers, because there hath not been an exact succession of prophets since that time."—*Contra Apion*, I : 8.

Ezra and Nehemiah and the "received text" of our Lord's day, except as to the order of arranging the books.

13. *The Hebrew order* varied, but the following is a common one:

I. *Pentateuch.*—Genesis, Exodus, Leviticus, Numbers, Deuteronomy.

II. *Earlier Prophets.*—Joshua, Judges, 1 and 2 Samuel, 1 and 2 Kings.

III. *Later Prophets.*—(*a*) Greater: Isaiah, Jeremiah, Ezekiel. (*b*) Lesser: Hosea, Joel, Amos, Obadiah, Jonah, Micah, Nahum, Habakkuk, Zephaniah, Haggai, Zechariah, Malachi.

IV. *K'tubim or Hagiographa.*—(*a*) Psalms, Proverbs, Job. (*b*) Five Rolls, Song of Songs, Ruth, Lamentations, Ecclesiastes, Esther. (*c*) Daniel, Ezra, Nehemiah, 1 and 2 Chronicles.

It will be observed that the Hebrew Old Testament closes with the Chronicles regarded as one book. This will throw light on the reference to "Abel and Zachariah" as the first and last-mentioned martyr (Matt. 23 : 35). An earlier Hebrew arrangement, it is held, existed, by which Ruth was a part of or appendix to Judges, and Lamentations to Jeremiah. The books of Samuel were one, as also the two books of Kings, and the twelve minor prophets one, thus making twenty-four books in the Hebrew Bible.

14. *Supposed Variations in the Lists of Books.*—The historical facts in favor of the authority of the Old Testament books now received by evangelical Christians, have not really been weakened by exaggerating the variations from that list. For example, it is asserted that there was (1) a *Sadducean*, (2) a *Samaritan*, and (3) an *Alexandrian* canon of the Old Testament. There is no historical proof that

G

the Sadducees received the books of Moses only, and did not receive the other Old Testament books. The Samaritan mixed population, which broke away from the Jews and set up a worship and temple on Mt. Gerizim, did restrict their Old Testament canon to the five books of Moses. The Alexandrian Jews, on the other hand, did put other books with the books of the ordinary Hebrew Old Testament, without distinctly marking the difference; but it is not proven that the mass of even those Jews accepted them all as of divine authority. Added to these three, are others more recent as:(4) the *Patristic* list, that grew out of the Alexandrian or Septuagint version, which failed to draw a sharp line between the canonical and apocryphal books. From this, again, came (5) the *Roman Catholic* canon. By the Council of Trent, 1546, it was declared that the larger canon including the Apocrypha was deserving of "equal veneration" with the other books; but later Romanists of intelligence have sought by various devices to escape from this decisive decree. On the same side some count (6) the *Greek Church*. But that church is divided on the question, or at least is not consistent in its edicts. The Synods of Constantinople, 1638, Jassy, 1642, Jerusalem, 1672, refused to distinguish the canonical from the apocryphal Old Testament books, although Cyril of Constantinople did so mark them. The Larger Catechism of that church, Moscow 1839, an authoritative doctrinal standard of the church in Russia, excludes the apocryphal Old Testament books on the ground that "they do not exist in Hebrew." The Old Catholic Union, 1874, declares "that the apocryphal or deutero-canonical books of the Old Testament are not of the same canonicity as the books contained in the Hebrew canon." They also say that no translation can have superior authority to the original text. (7) The *Protestant* canon conforms to the traditional Hebrew list, and is based on the most ancient and the highest authority. Luther translated the Old Testament apocryphal books and commended them for private reading, but did not count them of like divine authority with the books in the ancient Hebrew canon. The church of England allows the use of the apocryphal books "for example of life in instruction of manners: but yet doth it not apply to them to establish any doctrine." The Belgic Confession holds a similar position. The Westminster Confession expressly declares them to be of no more value than other human writings; "The books commonly called Apocrypha, not being of divine inspiration, are no part of the canon of Scripture; and therefore are of no authority in the Church of God, nor to be otherwise approved or made use of than other human writings." Chap. I. §3. The various evangelical bodies of Christians clearly agree in uniformly omitting the Apocrypha from the list of sacred books.

CHAPTER IX.

That part of the Bible which begins with the creation and ends with the death of Moses, in early times was written in one Hebrew roll, or book. In the Greek translation it was arranged in five books, as now in our English Bibles.

1. *Name.*—These five books are often called " The Pentateuch," from the Greek ὁ πεντάτευχος (*ho pentateuchos*), meaning "*the five-volumed*" book. The Hebrews call it *Torah*, "Law," and, more fully, "The Law of Moses." The unity of this entire portion of the Scriptures is founded upon history and the close continuity of the contents of the books. For example, in Hebrew manuscripts, Genesis is reckoned not as one of five books, but as *one part* of *one* book. A Hebrew conjunctive word connects Exodus with Genesis, as it does each of the five books except Deuteronomy.

2. DIVISION.—The division into five books is ascribed by some to the Alexandrian translators (285 B.C.), and by others to the Maccabæan period, or possibly to the era of Ezra. The one roll, however, continued to be referred to as " The Law " even to the time of Christ; for under this title he quoted several of the first five books.[1] The title of

---

[1] Matt. 12 : 5, *e. g.*, refers to Numbers; Luke 10 : 26, 27 to Deuteronomy and Leviticus; Luke 2 : 22, 23 to Exodus and Leviticus, etc., but under the one designation, The Law.

each of the five separate books in our English version is
derived through the Latin from the Alexandrian Greek
version. These titles indicate the topic or contents of the
respective books. Genesis tells of the birth or creation of
the world; Exodus, of the exodus or departure of the Hebrews from Egypt; Leviticus, of the law or rules of worship;
Numbers, of the census of the people in the wilderness;
and Deuteronomy—meaning " the second law "—is a summary or re-statement of the law. The Hebrew title for
each of these books (when they note any division) was the
first words with which each book began. The writers often
referred to the roll as " Moses " or " The Law," and
pointed out the place by the first word or words of the
section, as " the bush," Luke 20 : 37, which is the phrase
there used to refer to the section in Ex. 3 : 6. This appears clearly in the Revised Version.

The Talmud and Ancient Jewish Bibles divided " The
Law " into fifty-four sections called *Perashioth ;* and these
were again subdivided into smaller sections and classed
under two heads, " Open " sections, and " Shut." These
were marked by P or S to catch the reader's eye. Possibly
this is the origin of the " ¶ " in modern Bibles. One of
these longer sections was to be read each Sabbath of the year.
Broadly, then, Genesis may be called the book of *beginnings;*
Exodus, the book of *deliverance ;* Leviticus, the *priestly*
book ; Numbers, the book of *marches and of wars ;* Deuteronomy, the *statute* or *code* book of the Hebrew people.

3. *Authorship.*—The uniform historic testimony of early
Christian, of Hebrew and of heathen writers is that Moses
was believed to be the writer of the Pentateuch or first
five books of the Bible. This view has been held, practically without question, until comparatively recent times.

The Talmud says, "Moses wrote his book, the Pentateuch, with the exception of eight verses, the last eight verses, which were written by Joshua." Philo and Josephus held that these books were written by Moses. "Newer criticism" has reopened the question. It concedes that Hebrew testimony and tradition say Moses was the author; but is tradition right? or was the "Law" compiled by Samuel, Solomon, Josiah, Ezra, or by some unknown "redactor" of a later period?[1] These theories have been varied, progressing from one hypothesis to another, or disagreeing among themselves as to the authorship and composition of the books.

Astruc (1760) held that Genesis was composed of two different documents by two writers. Then this "documentary" character was declared to run through the three books following Genesis; the documents being loosely put together. Then came a "fragmentary" theory, which pushed aside the documentary one. It was claimed that the "Elohistic" portion was the possible basis, but that there was a multitude of other fragments. This was again changed to the view that the three or more so-called original "documents" were themselves composite works, and were wrought into one composite work by some unknown "redactor," and probably two or three successive "redactors." No sooner are the difficulties of the position on one theory shown than objectors shift to another theory.[2]

---

[1] Ben Ezra, of the twelfth century, feebly raised this inquiry. It was revived by Carlstadt, Spinoza, Astruc, Eichhorn and Hupfeld. These have been followed by Bleek, Graf, Wellhausen, Robertson Smith and others of the more or less destructive and radical schools of critics. It is not unfair to charge that the tendency of this criticism is to deny or minify the divine element, the supernatural, in the Scriptures.

[2] In general it may be stated that according to this "newer criti-

Closely related to the author and mode of composition of the five books is the *date* of these several portions. Some have urged that the "priestly code" (Elohistic) was the oldest; others have as stoutly maintained that it was the newest and surely belonged to the post-exilic era.

4. *Composition.*—This uncertain *sea of speculation* may be left to its own tossings. Aside from inferences, what do the books definitely say respecting their authorship and composition?

(1) .There is no definite avowal of authorship that can surely apply to the entire Pentateuch; but it must apply to a very large portion, especially of the code. For example, God commanded Moses to write the words of the covenant (Ex. 34 : 27); Moses declared these words to Israel (Ex. 35 : 1). Again, it is declared in Deut. 31 : 24, 26, that "when Moses had made an end of writing the words of this law in a book, until they were finished, that Moses commanded the Levites, . . . Take this book of the law, and put it in the side of the ark of the covenant of the Lord your God." This is a distinct assertion that Moses was the writer of some Hebrew code of laws.

(2) The whole history is chiefly given in the third person. "The Lord spake unto Moses" frequently occurs. "And Moses commanded," "Moses said," or "the words of Moses," are other expressions frequently found in the Pentateuch.

(3) Deut. 34 records the death of Moses. This was added by a later hand (see "unto this day" of v. 6), probably during the period of the judges.

---

cism" the Pentateuch was composed in three or more portions, called the Elohistic, Jehovistic and Deuteronomic.

(4) The five books contain several remarkably graphic and interesting biographies. Yet obviously the main purpose of these books is not biography, nor personal or local history. The object is clearly to record the origin of the Hebrew people and to chronicle their early national annals.

(5) Is this form not the one most suitable for national annals? Indeed, if these books were intended as authentic theocratic records of the origin of the race, and of the Hebrew nation in particular, would not the *impersonal* form be the most natural one? In official annals of government, the identity of the writer is of smaller importance than the authenticity of the record. Moses, as the great lawgiver of Israel, would be expected to leave some authorized copy of the laws received for the people. Hebrew writers say he did leave such a record in the Pentateuch. There is nothing in the books themselves against their general Mosaic authorship. There are many incidental evidences in favor of it,—particularly that they were written as national annals by direction and authority of Moses; the death of Moses being added by an authorized successor. Since, however, the discussions respecting the composition and date of the Pentateuch are pressing upon popular attention, a few leading points may be helpful in showing the character of the conflict.

5. *Against the traditional view*, beside the literary and linguistic argument, the newer criticism urges—(1) That the Pentateuch sanctions one central place of worship. But it is said that several places were allowed up to the time of Josiah. To this it may be said, one, the tent, prevailed in the wilderness. (2) Leviticus requires priests to be of the family of Aaron, while Deuteronomy and Judges ap-

pear to treat Levites as priests. (3) The Levitical cities named in the Pentateuch, it is asserted, are not to be found as such in history. (4) The feasts were not observed as the Pentateuch required. (5) The details of the narrative and history of the Hebrew worship are said to be against the early Mosaic date.

6. *In favor of the antiquity and Mosaic authority of the Pentateuch* is urged—(1) The uniform testimony of past ages, as already noted. It is remarkable that a non-Mosaic origin and a late date for the Pentateuch should be left for a few recent critics to discover, and throws suspicion upon the theory.

(2) The use of any existent documents that were accessible in composing the theocratic history in the Pentateuch does not impair the divine authority, or Mosaic authorship, of the books. But the critics cannot agree upon criteria that will enable us to determine definitely any of these fragments; hence they cannot demonstrate that any were incorporated, though they may have been used in composing the Mosaic books.

(3) If the books were written as the destructive critics claim, it is difficult to clear the authors of literary fraud. It is well-nigh inconceivable that writings cast in such a high moral, solemn and spiritual tone could be written by those who would deliberately deceive readers.

(4) There is no historic evidence of the existence of separate documents. The opposers to the Mosaic origin of the books have had no agreement among themselves about them. They do not agree upon the number or limit of the original "fragments," nor upon their age. Those that are claimed as latest by some are also asserted to contain some earliest records by others.

(5) The Hebrew people must have had laws and a history for ages previous to the exilic period. The new theory of the Pentateuch leaves them practically without either. The records of the five books of Moses, however, fit well with what we know of Egypt and other nations in the Mosaic era. Grant for a moment that this is not history: here stands Moses, the greatest name in ancient records as lawgiver, reformer and general, to be accounted for. How did he get into history?

(6) Early Hebrews, though enslaved in Egypt, were not a savage horde. The monumental records of the Mosaic age constantly coming to light are confirming the civilization existing in the land where they dwelt and the accuracy of the Mosaic records.

(7) The weight of literary and linguistic facts, in truth, tells strongly for the Mosaic composition and antiquity of the Pentateuch. The language has an infusion of Egyptian words; yet the system of religious worship is in sharp contrast with Egyptian sacrifices and worship. The place of worship is the tent (tabernacle); excommunication is to be "cast out of the camp;" the scapegoat goes into the wilderness; all the ritual speaks of the wandering life, consistent with the belief that the main portion of the Pentateuch was written at the period and in the region where it professes to have been written. The ark had the law; and the ark certainly dates to the wilderness life.

(8) Finally, the archaic quality in the language of the Pentateuch is marked; the apparent tinges of a later speech are too few to weigh against the weightier evidence for the antiquity of the writing. Recent discoveries are increasing the proofs for the Mosaic age and composition; while all the material objections of modern criticism can be ex-

plained upon the Mosaic theory. The objectors are beset
with more numerous and far greater difficulties. They
must reconstruct Hebrew history, account for the long-
existing belief in regard to that history as popularly accepted, and explain the monumental and other records
which fit well into Hebrew history as hitherto understood,
and which imply the early existence of the Hebrew people
in conditions similar to those described in the Mosaic
books.

(9) The change in the style and character of the latter
portion of the Pentateuch, in comparison with the first, is
readily accounted for by the supposition that forty years
intervened between the composition of the first portion,
up to the report of the spies and the consequent judgment,
and the latter, including the Deuteronomic portion. The
writer, after forty years of added experience, would naturally take on new forms and expressions in his composition.

(10) The annals bear marks of being composed at or near
the period of their occurrence. A writer making such a
record centuries later would almost surely fall into errors
and anachronisms which the earlier monumental records
would expose. Such a composition without errors would
itself be a greater miracle than the gift of supernatural
guidance by divine inspiration.

(11) The New Testament evidence cannot be blown
aside by a breath. Jesus says of Moses, " He wrote of
me " (John 5 : 46, 47). So also, " beginning at Moses,
. . . he," etc. (Luke 24 : 27). The conclusion then is
that the historic evidence respecting the Mosaic authorship
and antiquity of the first five books of the Bible is entirely
trustworthy, and modern research and adverse criticism

have caused new and yet stronger evidence to be brought to light in support of that view.[1]

---

[1] The literature on this subject is abundant. Those who desire a brief statement of the Wellhausen theory, which just now is prominent in the disintegrating schools of criticism, may refer to the article "Pentateuch" in the *Encyclopædia Britannica*, 9th ed. For the evangelical view, see Bissell's *Pentateuch : its Origin and Structure*, 1885; also Pentateuchal discussions, Profs. Harper, Green and others, in *Hebraica*, vols. v. and vi., 1889–90.

CHAPTER X.

Grouping the Old Testament books according to their contents, there are twelve almost wholly historical. In the order of the books found in English Bibles these twelve historical books follow the five books of the law. They begin with Joshua and end with Esther.

1. *Hebrew Order.*—In the Hebrew Bible six of these books, from Joshua to 2 Kings inclusive (not counting Ruth), are in a separate division called "Earlier Prophets." They were so named by the Massorites, because these books recount the deeds of prophets, and Jewish tradition declared that they were written by prophets. The other six historical books are placed in the last division, the Hagiographa of the Hebrew Bible, following the Psalms, Ruth having the 5th place in that division, Esther the 8th, Ezra the 10th, Nehemiah the 11th and the Chronicles the last and closing one of the Hebrew Scriptures.

2. *Period Covered.*—These twelve historical books cover about 1000 years of Hebrew history from the death of Moses to the restoration and rebuilding of the temple after the great exile. This history of ten centuries may be divided into three unequal periods: from the death of Moses to Saul, about 350 years; from Saul's accession to the fall of Samaria, about 375 years; from the fall of Samaria to the restoration of the temple and Jerusalem after Nehemiah,

(101)

about 300 years. Or, again, the era covered by the historical books may be divided into—(1) the Conquest of Canaan (Joshua); (2) The Rule of Judges (Judges, Ruth and 1 Sam. 1 to 12); (3) The United Monarchy (1 Sam. 12 to 1 Kings 12, and 1 Chron. 1 to 2 Chron. 10); (4) The Two Monarchies (1 Kings 12 to 2 Kings 25 and 2 Chron. 10 to 36); (5) The Exile and Restoration (Esther, Ezra and Nehemiah). The books have little regard to periods in the history.

3. *Authors.*—The authors of the twelve historical books are not definitely known. According to Jewish tradition the chief writers of them were Joshua, Samuel, Jeremiah, Ezra and Nehemiah. Only a brief notice of each book can be given.

4. *Joshua* is so named from the exploits of the hero described in it, and not as a mark of authorship. Modern critics have grouped it with the five books of Moses, and called the whole "The Hexateuch." They would also date its composition near the exilic or even post-exilic era and by some unknown writer. Jewish and Christian tradition and reverent scholars assign its authorship to Joshua (except the last five verses), and say that it was composed at the period of the conquest by an eye-witness, and from documents of that time. See for example the address of Joshua in chaps. 23, 24, and the record of his interviews with Jehovah, chaps. 1, 3, 5, 7. The few single clauses which destructive critics urge as proving a later date may have been marginal notes by Samuel or some prophet of Saul or David's time. They fail to prove a later composition of the book. A careful study of Joshua is the best foundation for a right mastery of Hebrew history.

5. *Judges.*—This book is so named because it records

the deeds of some of the early judges (about thirteen) who were raised up to deliver Israel from the oppression of hostile nations and tribes on its borders. The length of the period covered by this book is variously computed from 250 to 450 years. The supposed reference to the length of this period in the speech of Paul (Acts 13 : 19, 20) is now generally regarded as referring not alone to the period of the judges, but to the possession of the land from the Abrahamic promise to Joshua. "He gave *them* their land for an inheritance, for about four hundred and fifty years: and after these things he gave *them* judges until Samuel" (Acts 13 : 19, 20, Revised Version). It is evidently a book of annals. The author is not known, though the Talmud ascribes it to Samuel, and this is a popular belief. It appears to have been gathered from various documents, to impress moral and religious lessons. The difficulties of the book are the chronology, apparently two introductions, and the adjustment of the rule of the several judges. It contains some of the most deeply interesting biographical sketches in the Old Testament. The reader never wearies of the stories of Gideon, Samson, Deborah and Jephthah.

6. RUTH.—The book itself fixes the period when the beautiful heroine lived. It was "in the days when the judges ruled" (Ruth 1 : 1). But this does not fix the date of its composition. Unless the closing verses were added by another than the original author, it cannot have been written before the time of David. In the Hebrew Bible it is placed as the fifth book after the Psalms. In the Septuagint it follows Judges, as in English Bibles. Historically it may be counted an appendix to Judges and an introduction to the books of Samuel. It may have been written

by Samuel, as one Jewish tradition asserts.   The Aramaisms, which are supposed by some to indicate a later date,
are represented as spoken by foreigners and are not in the
language of the author.   They are not conclusive against
an early date.   Nor is the mention of "plucking off the
shoe" against, but rather in favor of, its composition as
early as the period of David.   The book is a touching and
dramatic picture of domestic life in that period.

7. SAMUEL.—The two books of Samuel were originally
one in the Hebrew Bible.   Even the Massoretic note at the
end of the second book, giving the number of verses, treats
them as one book.   The Septuagint regarded the books of
Samuel and of Kings as a complete history of the Hebrew
kingdom, and divided them into four, calling them "Books
of the Kingdoms."   This division is followed in the Latin
and Douay versions, where they are named the 1st, 2d, 3d
and 4th Books of Kings.   The division was introduced
into Hebrew printed Bibles in 1518.

The *author* of the first two, now called 1 and 2 Samuel,
is unknown.   The name of the books probably arises from
the fact that Samuel is the hero of the first part.   Samuel
could have written only twenty-four chapters of the first
book, since the twenty-fifth chapter records his death.
The contents indicate that official records may have been
consulted by the writer, and national hymns were incorporated in the work, as the song of Hannah (1 Sam. 2 : 1–
10); David's song over Abner (2 Sam. 3 : 33, 34); his
thanksgiving song, and his farewell song (2 Sam. 22 ; 23 :
1–7).

The *date* of composition was not later than Solomon s
time, as the language proves.   "It is pure Hebrew,
free from Aramaisms and late forms.   Constructions such

as are found in Kings are not found in Samuel."[1] The difficulties are not important, being the adjustment of the chronology, the variations between the Hebrew and Greek texts, and the *apparent* discrepancies, as 1 Sam. 23 : 19 ; 24 : 22, and ch. 26.

8. KINGS.—The two books of Kings (one in Hebrew) are a continuation of the history in the books of Samuel. The author is not certainly known. Jewish tradition names Jeremiah, and the language and style favor the tradition. Later scholars have conjectured that the author was Ezra or Baruch. The writer used existing records, as "Acts of Solomon," "Chronicles of the Kings of Judah" and "Chronicles of the Kings of Israel" (1 Kings 11 : 41; 14 : 19, 29). Yet there is a unity, a peculiar plan and symmetry of purpose in the books, indicative of a well-wrought work, and not a mere compilation. The *date* cannot be earlier than the exile. It probably belongs to the last half of the period of the exile. Recent Assyrian discoveries have thrown much new light upon the various dynasties mentioned in the books. The obscurities are not many nor important, and scholars have suggested various reasonable explanations. These books close the "Earlier Prophets" of the Hebrew Bible.

9. CHRONICLES.—These two books were also originally one, and are placed at the end of the Hebrew Bible. The Hebrew title is "The Diaries" or "The Affairs of the Times." The Septuagint calls them "*Paralipomena*," or "Things Omitted," under the erroneous idea that they were intended to supply omissions in the history in the four books of Kings. Jerome named them "Chronicles," and

---

[1] Prof. O. S. Stearns, *Introduction to the Old Testament*, p. 37.

7

was followed by Luther and by the English translators. Their *composition* is ascribed to Ezra by Jewish and Christian tradition, and in language and style they resemble the book of Ezra. The Chronicles are clearly independent history, not written to supply omissions in Kings, but to give the returned exiles information needful for them in re-settling the land of Canaan. The tribal and family descent would be very important in settling inheritances. Critics who wish to fix the composition of the Pentateuch after the exile have very sharply, but most unsuccessfully, assailed the books of Chronicles. The accounts of the temple service, the covenant, the reforms under Josiah and Hezekiah, are strong confirmations of the earlier origin of the Pentateuch. The *date* of Chronicles cannot be fixed earlier than the restoration from exile ; and as the history ends with the decree of Cyrus, that may be assumed as the time of their composition. Much of the work is evidently based upon existing and apparently official documents. For example, the first nine chapters appear to cite tribal genealogical records ; and in chaps. 23–26 the priestly records seem to be the basis of the history. In fact, eleven sources are distinctly named: "the book of Samuel the seer," "of Nathan the prophet," "of Gad the seer," "the prophecy of Ahijah," "the visions" or "the story" of "Iddo the seer against Jeroboam," another by him "concerning genealogies," "the book of Shemaiah the prophet," "the book of Jehu," "the book of the kings of Israel," "the book of the kings of Israel and Judah," and a book by Isaiah ; see 1 Chron. 29 : 29 ; 2 Chron. 9 : 29 ; 12 : 15 ; 13 : 22 ; 16 : 11 ; 20 : 34 ; 26 : 22 ; 27 : 7 ; 32 : 32. These numerous references to existing books containing more full records of the events very briefly mentioned in

the Chronicles show how abundant were the written
sources to which the author had access, and how familiar
he was with the contents of those original records.   They
tend strongly to confirm the trustworthiness of his
chronicle ; and this being maintained, the strongest attacks
of the newer criticism will fall or can be effectively repelled.

   10. EZRA.—This book in the Hebrew Bible is the tenth
after the Psalms.   The Jews (Josephus and the Talmud),
Origen and Jerome, regard Ezra and Nehemiah as one
book in two parts.   But Nehemiah has its own title in Hebrew.   The two books are called Esdras and Nehemiah
in the Septuagint, and 1 and 2 Esdras in the Vulgate.
Historically Ezra follows close after Chronicles ; hence the
order in our Bibles is in better accord with the contents
than the order in Hebrew Bibles.   The author, according
to the Jews, was Ezra.   Modern critics admit that he wrote
a portion, but deem the whole a compilation by some unknown though contemporaneous writer.   A portion of it is
written in Chaldee or Aramaic, e. g., chaps. 4 : 8 to 6 : 6
and 7 : 1–26 ; but these are probably from public records.
The varying use of the first and third persons in the last
portion of chaps. 6 to 10 has a parallel in Daniel and Isaiah.
The writer in the latter case speaks of himself historically ;
in the former he writes of events which he witnessed.   That
Ezra was the author has been fairly sustained.   The date must
be placed in the fifth century before Christ, in the age of Cyrus, etc., and after Ezra's return to Jerusalem with the exiles.

   11. NEHEMIAH.—This book is the eleventh in order after
Psalms in the Hebrew Bible.   The author of the first seven
chapters was surely Nehemiah, for it is so avowed in the
book itself.   The writer of chaps. 8–13 is questioned by
many, although Keil accepts Nehemiah as their author.

The objections urged against his authorship of this portion
are that the narrative changes to the third person, and Nehemiah is spoken of as "Tirshatha" (Neh. 8 : 9), and that
the name of Jaddua appears as high priest (Neh. 12 : 1–
26), who lived in the time of Alexander, a century later
than Nehemiah.   But the other portions of chap. 12 and
chap. 13 are usually credited to Nehemiah.   The language
of the book has a strong infusion of Aramaisms and of words
of Persian origin.   After an interval of about twelve years,
it carries on the history of Ezra for about thirty years, until the temple of Zerubbabel was rebuilt.   It is the latest of
the historical books of the Old Testament.

   12. ESTHER.—Historically   this   book   belongs to the
period of the exiles, previous to Nehemiah and a portion
of Ezra.   Some regard it as an episode in the history of
those Israelites that did not return from exile, and an illustration of their moral decline.   The incident related in the
book of Esther gave rise to the feast of Purim, still cele-
brated among the Jews.   This book is the eighth following
the Psalms in the Hebrew Bible.   It appears to have been
regarded as an appendix to the history of the exilic period,
as Ruth was to Judges, and hence in the Septuagint was
added to Ezra and Nehemiah.   It does not contain the
name of God.   Perhaps the   name   was   intentionally
omitted, so that the book could be read at a joyous
festival without irreverence.   It forcibly illustrates God's
providence.   The author, some say, was Ezra; others say
Mordecai.   The date cannot be definitely stated, although
the events surely occurred between 480 and 430 B.C.   As it
seems to have been written by an eye-witness, internal evidence favors Mordecai as author and 480 to 470 B.C. as the
date.   The book contains many Persian words; but the

literary character is high, and the style lively. The summary execution of Haman and the sudden elevation of Mordecai find frequent illustrations in later history of Oriental courts.

13. These twelve books of the Old Testament contain the richest history of a race. Written by men illumined by the Holy Spirit, the grand purposes of God's providence are unfolded with marvellous compactness and clearness. The long succession of bloody struggles, the astonishing deliverances of God's people, their weak and wicked relapses into sin, the glorious power of Jehovah manifested to them, and preparing them for the future advent of Messiah, the promised Redeemer, give diversity and charm to the history and instruction to the devout mind.

Of the purpose and mission of the two Testaments Mr. Gladstone says:

14. GENERAL CHARACTER.—"As the heavens cover the earth from east to west, so the Scripture covers and comprehends the whole field of the destiny of man. The whole field is reached by its moral and potential energy, as a provision enduring to the end of time. But it is marvellous to consider how large a portion of it lies directly within the domain of the Old Testament. . . . The corroborative legends of Assyria, ascertained by modern research, concerning the Creation and the Flood, to which we know not what further additions may still progressively be made, carry us up, it may be finally said,

"'To the *first* syllable of recorded time.'

"Historic evidence does not warrant our carrying backwards the probable existence of the Adamic race for more than some such epoch as from 4000 to 6000 years anterior to the advent of Christ. And if, as appears likely, the Creation story has come down from the beginning, the Christian may feel a lively interest in observing that, for by far the larger portion of human history, the refreshing rain of divine inspiration has descended, with comparatively short intervals, from heaven upon earth, and the records of it have been collected and preserved in the Sacred Volume. Apart from every question of literary form and of detail, we now trace the probable origins of our Sacred Books far back beyond Moses and his time. And so we have a marvellous picture presented to us, not only all-prevailing for the imagination and the heart of man, but as I suppose quite unexampled in its historical appeal to the human intelligence. The whole human record is covered and bound together in that same unwearied and inviolable continuity, which weaves into a tissue the six Mosaic days of gradually advancing creations, and fastens them on at the hither end to the advancing stages of Adamic, and, in due course, of subsequent history.

"We find then that, apart from the question of moral purity and elevation, the Scriptures of the Old Testament appear to be distinguished from the sacred books possessed by various nations in several vital particulars. They deal with the Adamic race as a whole. They begin with the preparation of the earth for the habitation and use of man. They then, from his first origin, draw downwards a thread of personal history. This thread is enlarged into a web as, from being personal, the narrative becomes national, and eventually includes the whole race of man. They are not given once for all, as by Confucius or Zoroaster in their respective spheres; they do not deliver a mere code of morals or of legislation, but they purport to disclose a close and continuing superintendence from on high over human affairs. And the whole is doubly woven into one: first, by a chain of divine action, and of human instructors acting under divine authority, which is never broken until the time when political servitude, like another Egyptian captivity, has become the appointed destiny of the nation; secondly, by the Messianic bond, by the light of prophecy shining in a dark place, and directing onwards the minds of devout men to the "fulness of time" and the birth of the wondrous Child, so as effectually to link the old sacred books to the dispensation of the Advent, and to carry forward their office until the final day of doom. May it not boldly be asked, what parallel to such an outline as this can be supplied by any of the sacred books preserved among any other of the races of the world? So far, then, the office and work of the Old Testament, as presented to us by its own contents, is without a compeer among the old religions. It deals with the case of man as a whole. . . . It is a history of sin, and of redemption."

CHAPTER XI.

1. *The Oriental mind* delights in figures, metaphors and in brilliantly-imaginative forms of speech. The Hebrews were also in surroundings exceedingly favorable for sublime poetic creations. Poetry was their delight from the earliest beginnings of their history. More than one third of the entire Old Testament is poetry. Its poetry is among the oldest, the purest and the most sublime in the world. It is fitted to stir the deepest spiritual nature of man in all ages. In other languages much of the poetry relates to the temporal interests of the people; Hebrew poetry is truly the daughter of religion.

2. *Forms of Hebrew Poetry.*—Strictly there is neither epic nor dramatic poetry in Hebrew. The reason is obvious. Epic poetry springs from an effort to glorify human greatness—the heroic in man; the Hebrew was taught to glorify God. Hebrew poetry is almost wholly lyric and didactic, and some add also gnomic. There are no lyrics in the world comparable with the Psalms of David, no gnomic poetry equal to the Proverbs, and no didactic poem so perfect in form, so profound and majestic in thought or so exalted and spiritual in conception as the book of Job.

3. *Rhyme* and metre, common in modern poetry, are seldom found in Hebrew. Josephus tried to find hexameters in the songs of Ex. 15 and Deut. 32, and trimeters or

(112)

pentameters in the Psalms. Eusebius sought an heroic measure of sixteen syllables; while Jerome represented Job as written in dactyls and spondees, comparing Hebrew poetry with the Greek poems of Pindar, Alcæus and Sappho. Later scholars, as Sir W. Jones, Grove and Saalchütz, have applied similar rules; but no such system of metres can be found in Hebrew on any method of vocalizing now known, nor without destroying the Massoretic pointing. Bickell would make it conform to the Syriac, which is plausible, but has not found much favor with scholars.

4. *Parallelisms.*—Hebrew poetry, as Lowth and others have shown, consists chiefly of parallelisms and a certain swing and balance in their sentences which give an indescribable charm to their poetic compositions.

The parallelisms in Hebrew have been roughly divided into three kinds: (1) *Synonymous,* that is, where each line of the distich or tristich has the same thought, but in varied expression ; (2) *Antithetic,* where the thought of the second member of the parallelism is in contrast with that of the first ; and (3) *Synthetic,* where the thought is cumulative upon the same topic.

5. *Alliteration* and assonance are frequently used in Hebrew poetry, and rhyme occasionally, but the latter seldom runs beyond two or three lines.

The Hebrew poetic writers delighted in the older and sometimes the fuller forms of words. They use not the learned or artificial, but the simpler and more archaic speech, giving strength and music to the movement of their sentences.

6. *Poetic Books.*—There are five so-called poetical books in the Old Testament: Job, Psalms, Proverbs, Ecclesiastes,

and Song of Solomon. But beside these, large portions
of other books are in poetic language. All the prophetical
books except Daniel are poetry. The girls of Shiloh sang
as they gathered grapes; the maidens of Gilead chanted
the story of Jephthah's daughter; the boys learned David's
song of lament over Jonathan, and hunters and shepherds
whiled away the tediousness of the hunt and watch, by
songs and the flute.[1]

7. *Early Songs.*—The earliest specimen of poetry in the
Old Testament is Lamech's Sword Song. Some of the
most noted of Hebrew songs, outside the poetical books,
are those of Moses and Miriam, of Balaam, Deborah and
Hannah. The following list, though incomplete, will be
helpful to the student:

Lamech's Sword Song.......Gen. 4 : 23, 24.
Noah's Song...............Gen. 9 : 25-27.
About Rebekah............Gen. 25 : 23.
Isaac's Blessings.. ....Gen. 27 : 27-29, 39, 40.
Jacob's Farewell...........Gen. 49 : 2-27.
Moses' and Miriam's Song....Ex. 15 : 1-19, 21.
War Songs, etc............Num. 21 : 14, 15, 17, 18, 27-30.
Balaam's Prophecies........Num. 23 : 7-10, 18-24; 24 : 3-9, 15-24.
Moses' Prophetic Song......Deut. 32 : 1-43.
Moses' Blessing........... Deut. 33 : 2-29.
Joshua to the Sun..........Josh. 10 : 12, 13.
Song of Deborah and Barak.Judg. 5 : 2-21.
Samson's Riddle Song.......Judg. 15 : 16.
Hannah's Magnificat...... .1 Sam. 2 : 1-10.
David's Song of the Bow....2 Sam. 1 : 19-27.
David's Song over Abner.....2 Sam. 3 : 33, 34.
David's Deliverance.........2 Sam. 22 : 2-51 (cf. Ps. 18).
David's Last Words.........2 Sam. 23 : 1-7.
David's Thanksgiving.......1 Chron. 16 : 8-36.

---

[1] See Reuss, Hebrew Poetry, Herzog's Enc.

Hezekiah's Song..............Isa. 38 : 10–20.
Jonah's Prayer Song.........Jonah 2 : 2–9.
Habakkuk's Prayer Song.....Hab. 3 : 2–19.

There are four original songs in the New Testament cast in the spirit of Hebrew poetry:

Magnificat.....................Luke 1 : 46–55.
Benedictus.....................Luke 1 : 68–80.
Gloria in Excelsis.............Luke 2 : 14.
Nunc Dimittis.................Luke 2 : 29–33.

8. THE PSALMS.—The book of Psalms in the Hebrew Bible was the first of the *K'thubim*, or "Writings." The Psalms, Proverbs and Job were regarded as pre-eminently poetical books, and the Massorites distinguished them by a peculiar accentuation. The Psalms were called "*Sepher T'helim*," or "Book of Praises." The Greeks called it "*Psalmos*," from which the English " Psalms " is derived.

9. *Groups of Psalms.*—The Psalms are counted as one book, but in the Hebrew Bible are divided into five collections, rather inaptly termed "books" in the Revised English Version.

The end of each of the first four "books" is indicated by a doxology.

The books are: (I.) Ps. 1–41; (II.) Ps. 42–72; (III.) Ps. 73–89; (IV.) Ps. 90–106; (V.) Ps. 107–150. The topics of the Psalms have been compared to an oratorio in five parts : (1) Decline of man ; (2) Revival ; (3) Plaintive complaint ; (4) Response to the complaint ; (5) Final thanksgiving and triumph.

This five-fold division of the Psalms is very ancient, but when or by whom it was made is uncertain. Some ascribe it to Nehemiah or his time ; it certainly is two or three centuries older than the Christian era. The division appears in the Septuagint. Why it was made is not clear. Some conjecture that it was in accord with the supposed chronological order of the Psalms, or was an arrangement according to authors, topics, or for liturgical use. The collection could not have been completed before the time of Ezra. About fifty Psalms are quoted in the New Testament.

10. *Authors.*—The titles or inscriptions of the Psalms are not by the original authors, but belong to an early age. They are attached to 101 psalms. The 49 not having titles, the Talmud calls "Orphan Psalms." According to these titles, 73 psalms are ascribed to David,[1] 12 to Asaph one of David's singers, 12 to the sons of Korah[2] a priestly family of singers of David's time, 2 (72d and 127th) to Solomon, 1 (90th) to Moses, and 1 (89th) to Ethan. The other 49 are anonymous. But the Septuagint assigns the 127th to Jeremiah, the 146th to Haggai, and the 147th to Zechariah. It is worthy of note that the great Hallel songs, Ps. 115–118, and the famous alphabetic hymn, the 119th, are among the anonymous songs.

11. *Classification of Songs.*—The most ancient classification, aside from the division into five collections, is also found in the titles. The meaning of these is obscure. Some are termed *Shir*, a solo for the voice; *Mizmor*, song of praise accompanied with an instrument; *Maschil*, ode or didactic song; *Michtam*, a catch-word poem (Delitzsch); *Shiggaion*, an excited ode; *Thephillah*, a prayer-song; *Shir jedidoth*,

---

[1] The Septuagint ascribes 85 psalms to David. The New Testament cites Pss. 2 and 95 as his. This reduces the number by anonymous writers to 34. But Delitzsch thinks only 50 can be defended as David's from internal evidence.

[2] If, however, Ps. 88 is ascribed to Hernan, as some render the title, then only 11 were by the sons of Korah.

a song of loves; *Shir hamma 'a loth*, a song of ascent or pilgrim songs; *Kinah*, dirge or elegy. Modern groups are based upon the contents, as seven (some say eight) penitential (6th, 25th, 32d [38th], 51st, 102d, 130th, 143d), seven imprecatory psalms (35th, 52d, 58th, 59th, 69th, 109th, 137th), pilgrim songs, psalms of thanksgiving, of adoration, of faith and hope, Messianic psalms, and historic psalms.

Some psalms have parallelisms or longer stanzas, each beginning with an initial letter corresponding to the twenty-two letters of the Hebrew alphabet. There are seven of these alphabetic psalms and five other alphabetic poems in the Old Testament. Some psalms are choral, as 24th, 115th, 135th; some gradational, as 121st, 124th. Of the psalms ascribed to David, several have Chaldaic or Aramaic forms that betray a later author.

12. *Proverbs.*—The Hebrew title to this book is *Mishle Sh'lomo*, "Proverbs of Solomon," so called from the introductory words. The Hebrew word for proverbs is used in a variety of meanings, as pithy saying, parable, aphorism or maxim, and for more extended illustration. (See Micah 2 : 4; Hab. 2 : 6; 1 Sam. 10 : 12; Prov. 1 : 1; Eccles. 12 : 9; and Num. 23 : 7–10.) The soul of a proverb is brevity and great wisdom. It condenses the result of a life of wise observation and varied experience into a few words, a single parallelism. With Orientals it was and is popular, because easily remembered. Secular literature has several collections of proverbs, as the "Sayings of the Seven Wise Men of Greece," the "Golden Songs ascribed to Pythagoras," and Arabic proverbs. But the Proverbs of the Bible are unequalled in wit and wisdom. They abound in polished and sparkling gems of wisdom, bearing the stamp of in-

spiration (Prov. 1 : 7). The Proverbs are divided into seven parts: (1) chap. 1 : 1–6; (2) 1 : 7 to chap. 9; (3) chaps. 10 to 22 : 16; (4) 22 : 17 to chap. 24; (5) chaps. 25 to 29 ; (6) chap. 30 to 31 : 9 ; (7) chap. 31 : 10–31.

13. *Authors of Proverbs.*—The Proverbs are ascribed to Solomon,[1] and it is clear he wrote or compiled the most of them. Yet there were several other authors of the latter portion, as the men of Hezekiah, Agur, Lemuel. (See Prov. 1 : 1 ; 10 : 1 ; 25 : 1 ; 30 : 1 ; 31 : 1.)

14. *The date* of the complete collection is certainly not older than Hezekiah, though the greater portion was in existence from the time of Solomon.

15. *The Structure* is that of poetic parallelisms, in lines of single, double, triple or more couplets. The sense or thought is usually either synonymous or antithetic in these couplets. For example—

> " Happy is the man that findeth wisdom,
> And the man that getteth understanding " (3 : 13),

is synonymous in thought.

> " A wise son maketh a glad father:
> But a foolish son is the heaviness [grief] of his mother " (10: 1),

is an antithetic parallelism.

> " As a bird that wandereth from her nest,
> So is a man that wandereth from his place " (27 : 8),

is an instance of simple comparison.

> " Wine is a mocker, strong drink a brawler;
> And whosoever erreth [reeleth] thereby is not wise " (20 : 1),

---

[1] There is a Jewish tradition that Solomon composed the Song of Songs in his youth, Proverbs in mature manhood, and Ecclesiastes in his old age.

is an example of amplification of thought, containing a
reason for the warning.   (See also 3 : 3 ; 27 : 10.)

The book of Proverbs is the storehouse whence all Christians and some heathen peoples have drawn practical wisdom, and it teaches that the true source of wisdom is Jehovah.

16. JOB.—This book is so named not as indicating the
author, but the hero.

Author.—The book itself does not indicate the author.
The Jews and early Christian writers ascribed it to Moses.
He was well fitted to write such a work, and in Midian
would be wont to meditate on such a theme.   The contents
in the main indicate that it was written before the priest-
hood, ceremonial worship and law were instituted.   Some
say the writer was Job.   Later scholars ascribe it to the age
of Solomon, chiefly on the ground that the artistic structure
presupposes higher training than the Mosaic period, and
that there are some Aramaisms and allusions to the Mosaic
law.   Advanced critics would assign it to the exilic age,
depending mainly on the linguistic peculiarities to support
their view.   Proofs from recent discoveries have appeared
of an exceeding high state of art and knowledge existing
in Assyria and in Egypt earlier than the Mosaic era, weak-
ening the argument for a late origin.   The Aramaisms may
be accounted for on the view that the book was written in
Edom, Arabia or the Euphrates valley, and the supposed
allusions to the Mosaic law are obscure, probably only coincidences of thought.   The language fits the eastern region.   Compare Moabite Stone inscription.   The *date* of
the book depends upon the authorship.

17. *The Structure of Job.*—It is a didactic, almost dramatic, poem, in five parts.   It might be counted a drama

of life, a tragedy with a happy and not a tragic end. The *dramatis personæ* or characters are Jehovah, Satan, Job, Job's wife and his children, Eliphaz, Bildad, Zophar and Elihu. The five parts are: (1) Prologue (chaps. 1, 2); (2) Interviews with three friends (3–32); (3) with Elihu (32–38); (4) with Jehovah (38–41); (5) Job's submission (41, 42).

18. *The object* of the book is not to solve the problem of evil, though it throws some side light upon it. It shows that all calamities do not come as judgments for sin. It teaches the doctrine of a future life. The main object is indicated by the prologue and the tart question of Satan, " Doth Job serve God for naught ? " The chief purpose of the book is to show that *true religion does not spring from any form of selfishness*. It also shows the rectitude of the divine government when the righteous are afflicted. Special trials do not imply special guilt. They may exhibit God's benevolent design toward the sufferer, and they are intended to beget submission to God's holy will.

19. *Is the Book History ?*—This is answered yes, strictly so, by Josephus, Jewish rabbins and early Christian writers. Some modern critics say decisively no, but a mere poetic creation. The more reverent, thoughtful scholars accept it as based on historical facts, embellished or draped by rich Oriental figures and inspired poetic descriptions. Job was an historic person (Ezek. 14: 14, 20; James 5: 11), eminent for faith and piety. The trials were real, the Satanic influence, the losses, the complaints, the restoration, were all historical, we may well believe. The construction of the poem, the order and forms of the thought are wrought out by the inspired poet, so as to show how human history is related to the divine purposes, for the comfort and instruction of suffering humanity in all ages.

20. *Ecclesiastes.*—This is the seventh book following the Psalms in the Hebrew Scriptures, where it is called *Koheleth.* It is a didactic poem, teaching that to obey God is the *summum bonum,* the highest good. In a series of poetic soliloquies the writer depicts the vanities of earthly things, and the eternal verities above the sun. It represents a soul perplexed and tinged with scepticism, in the spirit of moderate Hebrew faith reaching out after Jehovah and eternal blessedness.

21. *The author,* according to the general belief of Jews and Christians, was Solomon. It is not widely inconsistent with his age, knowledge, experience and language. The Aramaisms are not numerous, and he might acquire them from familiarity with foreign nations. Some modern scholars (as Ewald, Delitzsch and Ginsburg) suppose the author was of the exilic or post-exilic age, and personated Solomon. But Pusey, Tayler Lewis, Dean Milman and others maintain that it belongs to the age of Solomon. It gives the impressions of one who has had a long life of broad observation and of great folly. It must be admitted that the arguments against its Solomonic authorship are weighty, but the difficulties in the way of the later theory are also great.

22. *The Song of Songs.*—This is the Hebrew name of the fourth book after the Psalms. It means the most beautiful of songs, "which is Solomon's." It appears as a remarkable cantata in five parts: a drama celebrating the excellence and purity of true wedded love.

23. *The author* was almost universally conceded to be Solomon until the last century. This was based on the title to the book itself, the evident knowledge of Solomon, his reign and royalty. The linguistic forms found in it appear

8

also in the song of Deborah, in Job and in Amos. Those who deny that it was written by Solomon rely largely upon the internal and linguistic evidences to support their view. The book illustrates what is said of Solomon in 1 Kings, 4 : 33, and describes a regal state and glory which was true in the reign of Solomon.

24. *The structure* is variously defined. Some hold that it is an antiphonal song between two lovers, attended by a chorus; the Shulamite a shepherdess, and a shepherd her royal lover; that it describes (1) mutual love, (2) lovers seeking and finding each other, (3) the marriage, (4) a separation and return, (5) praises of lovers and love.

25. *Interpretations* have been many, chiefly along three lines: (1) allegorical, full of fancies of every sort; (2) the literal, a poetic representation of pure love; (3) the typical, that it represents the Church and Christ as her spotless Husband. Whatever may be the spiritual lessons that it illustrates, it graphically shows the Hebrew idea of true bridal and conjugal love. It is aromatic with the fragrance of spring flowers, singing birds, and the charms of a sweet and strong love. It is fitting that one book of Scriptures should breathe the joy, peace and beauty that spring from domestic life of human love, a symbol and reflex of that divine love Christ has for His people.

The prophecies, which are also poetry, must be treated under Prophetical Books.

CHAPTER XII.

1. *The Prophets* were a large class of religious teachers among the Hebrews. Many of them were inspired to interpret and declare the will of God to the people. Prophet, in the popular sense, means a person inspired to foretell future events. This was not the chief work of the Hebrew prophets; but it was to act as divinely authorized teachers of religion and of spiritual truth. It also designated one who recorded such teachings or prophecies. Moses was a prophet, and prophets existed from the earliest period.

Later, the schools of the Hebrew prophets sprang up in the time of Samuel. They were a professional class. Many of this class were not divinely inspired or authorized, but were false prophets (Jer. 14 : 14 ; 23 : 21 ; Ezek. 13 : 2 ; 22 : 28 ; Micah 9 : 11). True prophets were often called from outside of the professional class to declare the word of the Lord and to interpret his dealings with the Hebrew and other nations. They were even authorized to denounce the professional prophets for false teachings.

2. *The Great Work* of the true prophets may be divided into five historical periods or crises:—(1) To unify the nation in the age of Samuel; (2) To suppress Baal-worship and the worship of strange gods in the time of Elijah and Elisha; (3) To teach that righteousness was required to re-

tain God's favor, under Amos and the shepherd prophets; (4) That Israel was spared to secure a holy people for the Messiah, as in the age of Isaiah and his contemporaries; (5) That God wanted reformation of the heart, and not merely of outward national or personal manners, as in the age of Jeremiah to Malachi. The nation might be destroyed, but Jehovah still desired personal holiness and purity of heart.

3. *Prophetical Books.*—The great mass of the prophetic instructions to the Hebrew people has been lost. That which has been preserved may, however, contain the substance of the divine messages for more than a thousand years. The books which the Hebrews called the "Earlier Prophets" have already been considered. There remain sixteen books, which they called the "Later Prophets" (excepting Daniel),[1] and that are pre-eminently prophetical books. The prophecies in these books, except Daniel, Jonah, Haggai and some of Malachi, are poetry or poetic in form. Portions of them are among the finest lyrics in the language, as the prayer of Habakkuk, the Lamentations of Jeremiah, and the Messianic odes in the 52d and 53d chapters of Isaiah.

4. *Division.*—The sixteen prophetic books are divided into four Major or greater, and twelve Minor or lesser, prophets. The Major or greater, were not so called from any belief that they were greater in character or in importance, but simply because the length of their recorded prophecies was greater than those called Minor or lesser.

The prophetic books may also be grouped in periods, as —(1) Before the great captivity, Jonah, Joel, Amos, Hosea,

---

[1] Daniel was placed among the *K'thubim*, or "Writings," and in order ranked ninth after the Psalms.

Micah, Nahum, Zephaniah, Isaiah, Jeremiah and Habakkuk. (2) During the captivity, Daniel, Ezekiel and Obadiah (?). (3) After the captivity, Haggai, Zechariah
and Malachi. It will be convenient briefly to notice the
books in the order in which they are found in the
English Bibles.

5. ISAIAH.—The title means "Salvation of Jehovah."
The prophecies recorded under his name rank second in
quantity, being exceeded only by those of Jeremiah. The
latter has about one-tenth more matter than Isaiah.

Author.—Jewish and Christian tradition, the apocryphal
Old Testament books, Ecclus. 48: 24, 25, and Josephus,
say the book was by the prophet Isaiah. The work is quoted
in the New Testament as by Isaiah about 120 times, the
quotations being about equally divided between the earlier
and later prophecies. The style is conceded to be similar
by all competent critics; technical expressions and hymns
are common to both and peculiar. But Ewald assigned the
book to seven authors; some modern critics to many more.
Others say there were two, the first and a "pseudo" or
"deutero" Isaiah. Against the unity of authorship, it is
asserted that the writer of chapters 40 to 66 describes his
own cities in ruin, and therefore lived after the Babylonian
captivity, about 150 years after Isaiah's death; that he
names the future deliverer, Cyrus, and so wrote *post even-
tum;* that prophets did not usually "project themselves
into a distant future, filling their pages with details of that
future." This proves too much. To say that Isaiah could
not write prophecy which would prove to be true history, is
to deny all prophecy. Who was the "great unknown?"
This question is unsolved. There is no trace of him in
Hebrew history or tradition. The book is conceded to be

Scripture.   It is the nature of prophecy to look into the future as if it were present.   Surely the description of the servant of God who suffers and dies for the sins of his people as described in the 53d chapter, fits no other person in history as it does Jesus Christ.   It is then, not very material to the divine character of this prophecy whether it was spoken 750 or 450 years before Christ.   Whoever the author or authors, it was inspired of God and is of divine authority.

The Structure.—It consists of a series of predictions expressed with an unction, pathos, holy rapture and poetic majesty unequalled in literature.   The prophecies, which are poetry, are connected by narrative in prose.   The contents centre about three leading topics,—redemption promised, redemption provided, redemption accomplished.

6. JEREMIAH.—These prophecies were spoken by the son of Hilkiah, of a priestly family of Anathoth, a small town about three miles northeast of Jerusalem.   His prophecies extended over about forty years, and relate to the southern kingdom of Judah from the period of Josiah to Zedekiah (621 to about 585 B. C.).   The author of the book is held to be Jeremiah himself, though he dictated portions of it to Baruch the scribe, who wrote it out. (Jer. 36 : 4 ; 45 : 1.) The last chapter appears to be an appendix, probably by another prophetic author.

The structure is simple and rugged.   Jeremiah is a bold preacher of righteousness to a sinning people.   Some have likened him to Dante proclaiming coming judgments, and to the Trojan Cassandra.   He is the poet of desolation and sorrow, but also of restoration, brightening the general blackness of the storm.   Portions of the book were intended to instruct and comfort the Jewish captives at

Babylon, and later portions were warnings to foreign nations.

7. LAMENTATIONS, by the same prophet, were called *Echoh* ("How?") in Hebrew. It is composed of five pathetic elegies lamenting over the destruction of Judah and Jerusalem by the Chaldæans. The five are parts of one great theme. The first two poems are alphabetic. They consist of twenty-two stanzas, each beginning with a letter of the Hebrew alphabet. The third chapter has sixty-six verses, the first three beginning with the first letter of the Hebrew alphabet, and the second three with the second letter, and so on to the end. The fourth chapter is arranged similar to the first and second, except that the verses have two clauses each.

8. EZEKIEL.—His name means "God strengthens." He was of a priestly family, and a prophet during the Babylonian exile. He lived in captivity at Tel-Abib, on the banks of the river Chebar, about two hundred miles north of Babylon. The book of his prophecy is diffuse, artistic, and abounds in allegory, symbols and obscurity. Its difficulties caused the Jews to declare that no one should read it until thirty years of age. Jerome called it "an ocean and labyrinth of the mysteries of God." But the difficulties are chiefly those of exposition.

The methods of interpretation applied to Ezekiel may be designated as four:—(1) Allegorical, dangerous in tendency; (2) historical, essentially destructive; (3) symbolical, requires careful and guarded qualifications; (4) typical, the more safe method.[1]

9. DANIEL is not placed among the prophetical books

---

[1] See Stearns, *Intro. Books of O. T.*, 1889.

in the Hebrew Bible, but with the *K'thubim*, being the
ninth book after the Psalms.   Various reasons have been
offered to explain this, but the real ground is not known.

Author.—The book itself implies that it was written by
Daniel, the prophet of the captivity.   This is the testimony of 1 Macc. 1 : 54; 2 : 59, 60, confirmed by the book
of Baruch and the references in the New Testament.   Josephus also states the current belief of his time that it was
by Daniel, "one of the greatest of the prophets." (*Jew.
Wars,* 6 : 2, 1; *Antiq.,* 11 : 8, 5.)   Some modern critics
ascribe it to a pseudo Daniel of the Maccabæan age.   They
urge that it was not among prophetical books; is written
partly in Aramaic; is not mentioned in Ecclus. 49, which
notices some great prophets.   But that also omits Ezra and
Mordecai and the twelve Minor prophets (for 49 : 10 is
regarded as spurious).   Many of the historical difficulties
have been removed by late discoveries in the Euphrates
valley.   The objection to Daniel as the author, sprang at
first largely from a wish to get rid of the miracles and
prophecies it contains.   The testimony continues too
strong for the severest criticism seriously to weaken.   The
unity of the book is generally conceded.

In structure it is complex, partly history and partly
prophecy.   This may account for its position in the Hebrew
Bible.   Chapters 2 : 4 to 7 are in Aramaic; the other portions in Hebrew.   The introduction and the Aramaic portion are written in the third person.   This may be accounted for by the change in the matter; the former is history, the latter prophetic vision.

In interpreting the prophetical portion of the book,
the first empire is generally agreed to be the Babylonian,
but as to the other three, some combine the Medes and

Persians into one, while some divide them.   Others regard the prophecy as covering a wide sweep of the world-empires before and after Christ.

10. THE MINOR PROPHETS.—These twelve books are counted one in the Hebrew Bible.   The order there is the same as in English Bibles.   The Septuagint changes the order of the first six thus, Hosea, Amos, Micah, Joel, Obadiah, Jonah.   Among the twelve are the earliest and the latest of the prophetic books.   They exhibit wide diversities of style, thought and illustration.   Here is the uncultured herdman Amos, the erratic, passionate Jonah, the finished and elegant poet Habakkuk, and the cultured and graceful Joel.

11.—HOSEA means the same as Jehoshua, "salvation." Stanley calls him the Jeremiah of the northern kingdom (Israel).   His prophetic work covered at least fifty (some say seventy) years.[1]   His style is sententious and concise, his language original and often quaint.   Of the several modes of interpretation, there are—(1) The literal or modified literal, that the prophet actually married a profligate woman, or one that became profligate ; (2) That it was a vision which the prophet describes ; (3) That typically he states the relation of Israel to Jehovah as that of an unfaithful wife to a husband.   There are several references to this book in the New Testament.   See Matt. 2 : 15 ; 9 : 13 ; 12 : 7 ; Rom. 9 : 25, 26.

12. JOEL is pure Hebrew, easy-flowing, elegant and classical in style, having bold, sublime imagery, vividness and power of description, bearing the impress of high culture. All these point to an early period of the monarchy as its

---

[1] See Pusey, *Minor Prophets.*

date—not later than 800 B.C.   Peter cites a prediction
of Joel as fulfilled in the Pentecostal revival and gift
of the Holy Spirit.   Compare Joel 2 : 28–32 with Acts 2 :
16–21.

13.—AMOS was a herdman of Tekoa, a small town about
twelve miles south of Jerusalem.   His name means "bur-
den" or "burdensome."   His style is in strong contrast
with that of Joel, and yet it charms the reader by a certain rugged simplicity and even sublimity and freshness,
with imagery fragrant of the pasture and rural scenes.
The date of the prophecies and of the book probably
follows that of Joel (about 810 to 780 B.C.).   An old tradition, not very trustworthy, declares that he died a martyr's death.

14. OBADIAH.—The smallest of the prophetic books reminds the reader of the old feud between Jacob and Esau.
It is a sweeping declaration of judgment against Edom for
its unnatural conduct toward Judah in its day of misfortune.
The date is uncertain.   It turns on vs. 11–14.   Some place
it in 889–884 B.C. ; others 606–588 B.C. or later.   There is
a strong resemblance in this book to Jer. 49 : 7–21, where
there is a similar prophecy against Edom.

15. JONAH was of Gath-hepher, a town of northern Palestine between Nazareth and Tiberias.   The book is a simple, natural and graphic story, bearing the marks of true
history unless the reader discards miracles.   The miracle
of the "great fish" (it does not say "whale") has been
made the butt of ridicule by sceptics since the days of
Julian the Apostate.   As a type of Christ, the narrative of
Jonah must include the miracle of the fish, and Christ himself points to it as such a type.   (Matt. 12 : 39–41 ; Luke
11 : 29–32.)   The book reads like history.   It may be de-

nied a historic character, but only "on the ground that all records of the supernatural are unhistoric."[1]

16. MICAH was a prophet of the Mediterranean plains near Gath. He is generally assigned to a period between 758 and 698 B.C.; but some, depending on internal evidence, regard this as rather too early, and would place him as contemporary with Isaiah. His style is bold, energetic, sometimes vehement and abrupt. He abounds in images, and his sudden transitions and conciseness make his meaning often obscure. He was counted a Messianic prophet, and his predictions are caught up and echoed in the Song of Zacharias (Luke 1 : 72, 73), and by the chief priests of Jerusalem (Matt. 2 : 5, 6).

17. NAHUM is a poetic book of great sublimity and with a beautiful imagery. Says Professor Edwards, "In grandeur of style, in condensed energy, in elevation of sentiment and rapid transitions, and in a certain completeness of representation, Nahum stands, if not the first, yet near the first, of the Hebrew prophets." The writer was probably of Galilee, though some have thought he was from the valley of the Tigris. He gives a sublime picture of the invasion of foes and the desolation of Nineveh.

18. HABAKKUK.—His name means "embracing." He was a Levite, but from whence he came and where he lived are unknown. The theme of the book is the overthrow of Judæa by the Chaldæans, and then the overthrow of the Chaldæans. The style is strong and the thoughts original. Ewald says that he "is master of a beautiful style, of powerful description, and an artistic power that enlivens and orders everything with charming effect." Of his eloquent

---

[1] Prof. Barrows, *Intro. Study of the Bible*, London, p. 274.

and sublime prayer-song (chapter 3), upon the majesty of Jehovah, Bishop Lowth says: "This anthem is unequalled in majesty and splendor of language and imagery." From this book Paul cites the famous text "the just shall live by his faith" (Hab. 2 : 4; Rom. 1 : 17), which was caught up by Luther and became the ringing watchword of the great Reformation.

19.—ZEPHANIAH, according to the heading of the book, belonged to the period of the great revival under Josiah, 641–610 B.C. It has been called the great judgment hymn. That marvellous description beginning "The great day of Jehovah is near, . . . That day . . . of wrath" (Zeph. 1 : 14, 15), furnished the keynote to that sublime Latin hymn ascribed to Thomas of Celano (1250), *Dies iræ, dies illa*, esteemed the grandest hymn of the middle ages—a hymn more frequently translated than any other, yet never equalled, and which brings before us, with thrilling power, the final judgment as an awful impending reality.[1]

20. HAGGAI, a prophet of the restoration. His book is plain prose, in a series of four or five discourses. It relates to the repair of the Temple, 1 : 1–12; 2 : 10–20; to the glory of the second temple, 2 : 1–9, and Zerubbabel's triumph over his enemies, 2 : 20–23. The second chapter contains a distinct reference to Christ as the "desire of all nations;" or, "the desirable things of all nations." (Hag. 2 : 7.)

21. ZECHARIAH is accounted the second in order and the greatest prophet of the restoration. The thought is essentially Messianic throughout the book. The theme is one, but under two (some say five or six) heads. The authorship

---

[1] See Schaff, *Dictionary of the Bible*, p. 915.

has been sharply questioned, some ascribing it to Jeremiah, because of the passage in Matt. 27 : 9, 10; but lately this theory has been virtually abandoned.   Others would separate the book into many sections of different ages ; but the authority and inspiration of the book are admitted by all reverent scholars.   Testimony is strong in favor of the unity of authorship.   The Septuagint credits it to Zechariah. Christ and the New Testament writers recognize but one author for it.   The book has six specific references to Christ—Zech. 3 : 8 ; 6 : 12 ; 9 : 9 ; 11 : 12 ; 12 : 10 ; 13 : 7.

22. MALACHI, meaning " my messenger," is the closing prophet of the Old Testament.   The book " is broken up into Socratic aphorisms, abounds in ellipses, is crisp and terse."   It is- bold and denunciatory in its messages, yet consoles the believer by rich Messianic promises.   It distinctly foretells that Elijah will come as the forerunner of the Messiah.   Should the forerunner not come, or fail in his mission, the prophet threatens that Jehovah will come and "smite the earth with a curse."   And thus prophecy in the Old Testament closes with a terrific warning, awaiting the opening of the New Testament with an angelic song, the *Gloria in Excelsis.*

SUPPLEMENT.

CHAPTER XIII.

CIRCULATION OF THE BIBLE.

1. *Languages and Dialects.*—It is estimated that at the beginning of the nineteenth century, the Bible and portions of it, had been issued in less than fifty languages and dialects. These were chiefly European, with a few languages of Western Asia, Northern Africa and North America. The American Bible Society states that the Bible or portions of it are printed in 363 versions and 287 dialects.[1] In 1890, according to the Reports of the British and Foreign Bible Society, the Bible in whole or in part was translated and published in 510 versions, in upwards of 300 languages and dialects.[2] The work is distributed as follows :

In languages or dialects directly aided by the B. & F. Soc., 225
"   "   "   "   indirectly aided   "   "   "   65
In languages and dialects by other Societies (estimated),   100

Total languages and dialects in 1890   .   . 390

In 1889 there were portions of the Scriptures translated into four new languages not before having the Bible. The first eighteen centuries of the Christian era produced less than fifty new versions of the Bible. In eleven years, from 1878 to 1889, one society, the British and Foreign Bible Society, added over sixty new versions of the Bible. The same Society has been engaged in the translation and revision of the Bible in 166 languages.

2. *Distribution of the Bible.*—It has been computed that 60,000 copies of the Gospels were circulated among Christians by the end of the second century.[3] Origen multiplied copies of the sacred books

---

[1] Manual (Revised Ed.), Am. Bib. Soc., p. 35.
[2] See Report British and Foreign Bible Society, 1889, pp. 452 to 463, and Report for 1890. Also Bagster's "Bible in Every Land," which gives specimens of the Bible in about 300 languages and dialects. Also Reports, Mildmay Conference, pp. 414-428, and Exeter Mission Conference.
[3] Norton, Genuineness of Gospels, Vol. I., pp. 28-36.

by employing virgins skilled in calligraphy. Eusebius made fifty copies of the entire Bible by order of the Emperor Constantine. Great numbers of copies of portions were written out for private use. But before the invention of printing the multiplication of copies of the Bible was slow, tedious and expensive. When Luther issued his German Version of the Bible, 100,000 copies were sold within forty years, besides probably ten times as many portions of the Bible.[1] In three years after the issue of the Great Bible in England (1539) 21,000 copies were printed, and between 1524 and 1611 not less than 278 editions of Bibles and Testaments in English were printed. In two years, after 1611, five editions of King James' Version were printed, besides separate editions of the New Testament, and there are now known to be in existence over seventy different issues of 1611, issued about this time.[2]

In the first fifteen years of this century, private publishers in America issued 134 editions of the Bible, and sixty-five editions of the New Testament. In the first sixty-five years of this century, there were issued in this country about 600 different editions of the Bible, and 200 editions of the New Testament, besides 100 editions of the Scriptures in foreign languages, and 100 editions of portions of the Bible. Some of these editions had a very large circulation.

At the end of the first half of the nineteenth century there were over thirty firms in this country, some of them having a large capital, engaged in publishing Bibles and portions of it, and issuing not less than 400,000 copies annually. Of these more than 200,000 copies were large family Bibles. At the same period, it is estimated that the importation of Bibles from England equalled the combined issues of all the Bible Societies and private publishers of the United States.[3]

3. *Copies Circulated.*—Since the beginning of this century Bibles, Testaments and portions of the Bible have been issued as follows:

The British and Foreign Bible Society has issued Bibles,
Testaments, and parts . . . . . 125,000,000[4]
The American Bible Society has issued Bibles and Testaments . . . . 55,000,000[5]
Other Bible Societies have issued Bibles and Testaments about 45,000,000
Private publishers, of the world, have issued Bibles and Testaments (estimated) 60,000,000

Total circulation in nineteenth century . 285,000,000

[1] Schaff. Hist. Christ. Ch. Vol. VI., p. 350.
[2] Manual, Am. Bib. Soc., pp. 33, 34.
[3] Manual, Am. Bib. Soc., p 34.
[4] See W. Wright's report London Conf. Vol. I., p. 148. Reports British and Foreign Bible Soc., 1889, 1891.
[5] Report Am. Bible Soc., 1891, and Report of Penna. Bible Soc., 1891, p. 11.

But there are about 1,450,000,000 population in the world. If we count five persons to each family, all these copies would fall short by eight millions of giving one copy of a Bible or any portion of it to each family in the world.

4. *The total annual issues* of all the Bible and Mission Societies of the world number about 6,500,000 volumes. The yearly circulation of the entire Bible and portions by private publishers, has been estimated as equal to that of all the Bible Societies. But this is perhaps an over-estimate. Yet when the Revised New Testament of 1881 was issued Oxford had orders for 1,000,000 copies before it was published, and Cambridge for as many more. Over 2,000,000 copies were sold in London, and over 500,000 copies in New York and Philadelphia. None of these were issued by Bible Societies, but all by private publishing houses. Over twenty editions were reprinted within a year in the United States. In view of what leading presses like the Oxford and Cambridge Presses of England, and many similar publishers in England, America and Germany are doing, it is surely an under-estimate to place their united issues at one-half that of the Societies, or say 4,000,000 copies yearly. Yet this swells the annual supply of Bibles and portions of God's word to over 10,000,000 copies.

5. The copies of the Scriptures circulated in *heathen lands* during this century are said to exceed in number all that were in the world from Moses to Martin Luther.

In one year nearly 500,000 volumes of the Bible, in whole or in parts, were circulated among the Chinese, about 300,000 in India, 14,000 in Persia, 300,000 in Russia, 125,000 in Turkey, 137,000 in Italy, and 50,000 in Egypt and Madagascar. More than 100,000 copies of the Scriptures go into South American countries each year.

An enterprising Italian publisher lately began the issue of the Bible in serial numbers, at about one cent per number, which reached a circulation of over 50,000 copies by subscription on the first issue.

Of the different translations made for mission fields Asia has 95; Africa, 31; America, 24; and the Pacific Islands, 22.

CHAPTER XIV.

CARE OF BIBLE TEXT.

Chapters, Words and Letters.

1. To the statements on pp. 60, 61, it may be added that the Jews not only counted the books, sections and paragraphs in their Hebrew Scriptures, the Old Testament, but also marked the number of times the same word occurred in each paragraph, the middle verse or paragraph of each book, every verse where words were supposed to be changed, or something forgotten, any letters deemed superfluous, letters that were inverted, not pronounced, or did not hang perpendicular, and counted and recorded the number of each.

2. The Massoretes also noted how many times each letter occurred in the Hebrew Bible. Walton in his Prolegomena gives the table of the Massoretes:

LETTERS.				TIMES.	LETTERS.				TIMES.
א Aleph in Hebrew Bible				42,377	ל Lamedh in Hebrew Bible				41,517
ב Beth	"	"	"	38,218	מ Mem	"	"	"	77,778
ג Gimel	"	"	"	29,537	נ Nun	"	"	"	41,696
ד Daleth	"	"	"	32,530	ס Samekh		"	"	13,580
ה He	"	"	"	47,504	ע Ayin	"	"	"	20,175
ו Vau	"	"	"	76,922	פ Pé	"	"	"	22,725
ז Zayin	"	"	"	22,876	צ Tsadhe	"	"	"	21,882
ח Ilheth	"	"	"	23,447	ק Koph	"	"	"	22,972
ט Teth	"	"	"	11,052	ר Resh	"	"	"	22,147
י Yodh	"	"	"	66,420	ש Shin	"	"	"	32,148
כ Kaph	"	"	"	48,253	ת Tāu	"	"	"	59,343

When a word was found in the text with a small circle annexed to it, then a word they supposed to be the true one would be written in the margin.

3. The Massoretes had a cabalistic way of noting the number of the sections, words, letters and the like in the Hebrew text, as putting the number of a congregation in one verse and the number of animals in the next, and the two added together made the number of times the letter indicated occurred in the book or in the Old Testament. Then they noted that two verses of the law began with the letter *Mem*; eleven verses began and ended with the letter *Nun*; forty verses had the word " Lo " three times, and so on.

4. As a curious specimen of what this minuteness of the Massoretes stimulated others to do, it is said that some anonymous writer of the last century spent three years in counting and recording similar facts in respect to the Common English, or King James' Version of the Scriptures. As the English text varies in spelling and form, not having the fixed type of the old Hebrew, such a count of the English text must vary considerable, at different periods. The Revised English Version from various omissions of verses, portions of verses, and change of words in italics, which the English translators insert to make the sense clearer to the common reader, would vary more widely than would different editions of King James' Version. The compiler called his work *Old and New Testament Dissected*, and gave the following summary of the English Bible:

	Old Testament.	New Testament.	Total.
Books.....	39	27	66
Chapters..	929	260	1,189
Verses....	23,214	7,959	31,173
Words....	592,439	181,253	773,692[1]
Letters.....	2,728,110	838,380	3,566,490

The shortest and the middle chapter in the Bible is Ps. 117. The middle verse of the Bible is Ps. 118 : 8. The word *and* occurs in the Old Testament 35,543 times. The same word occurs in the New Testament 6,853 times. The word Jehovah occurs 6,853 times.

The middle book of the Old Testament is Proverbs. The middle chapter of the Old Testament, Job 29. The middle of the verses in the Old Testament is between 2 Chron. 20 : 17 and 2 Chron. 20 : 18.

The shortest verse in the Old Testament is 1 Chron. 1 : 25.

The middle book of the New Testament is 2 Thess.

The middle of the chapters of the New Testament is between the 13th and 14th chapters of Romans.

The middle verse of the New Testament is Acts 17 : 17.

The shortest verse in the New Testament and in the Bible is John 11 : 35.

---

[1] The American Bible Society Manual gives the total number of words in the English Bible, 773,746; and the total number of letters, 3,566,480. This is doubtless due to a different division, as counting some compounds as two words, which some Bibles print as one word.

Ezra 7 : 21 has all the letters of the alphabet except *j*.

There are several passages of some length alike, as Isa. 37 is like 2 Kings 19.

5. *The Greek words.*—In the Greek text of the first three Gospels, Matthew contains 18,370 words (Revised Greek Text, Oxford, 1881); Mark 10,981 words; Luke 19,496 words, a total of 48,847 Greek words in the three synoptic Gospels.

The Revised English New Testament according to Rev. Rufus Wendell (Student's Edition, Albany, 1882) contains:

No. of paragraphs.....................................1,128
No. of verses.......................................7,943
No. of words.......................................179,914

The total number of words belonging to each writer is as follows:

Paul (fourteen books).....50,649 Mark (one book).........14,854
Luke (two books)........49,865 Peter (two books)........ 3,966
John (five books) ....34,236 James (one book)........ 2,306
Matthew (one book)......23,407 Jude (one book).......... 631

6. *The vocabulary,* or number of *different* Greek words used by each writer, is much smaller. For example, while the total number of Greek words in the first three Gospels is 48,847, the number of *different* Greek words used by these three writers in the Gospels is only about 2400, of which Luke uses nearly 1800.

APPENDIX.

ANALYSIS AND QUESTIONS

CHAPTER I.

ANGLO-AMERICAN, AND KING JAMES VERSIONS, pp. 8–18.

1. What is the religion of three foremost nations of the world? In what six things are they foremost? Name the three nations.

2. What is the greatest book of these great nations? What are three distinguishing marks of the greatness of the Bible among them? From what is the title Bible derived in Greek? By whom was the Latin title first used? How? Who used it in a preface? Who first used it as a title to the Christian Scriptures?

3. What would a Mongolian, Malayan, and Christian wish to know about the Bible? What ought every Christian to know about the Bible? In what order is the history here traced? With what facts do we begin?

4. *Anglo-American Version.* What is one of the latest English Versions of the Bible called? When was it first printed? Why is it called the *Revised Version?* Why is the older one called the *Common Version?* [See note p. 8.] Why called *Authorized Version?* Was it ever formally *authorized?* Why called *King James Version?*

5. By whom was a revision of the Common Version suggested? When? By whom again proposed? In what year? When and by whom was a revision committee appointed? What convocation declined to join in it? When was an American committee appointed? How many men were employed upon the revision? How many were British scholars? How many were American? How many of these were active members? [See note p. 9.]

6. When was the revision completed? When issued? When was the whole Bible issued? How is this event characterized? How was the translation of the New Testament received? Was the same interest shown in the revised Old Testament?

7. What is the first reason given for revising the Common Version? What is the second? What is the third? How has a better text been attained?

(140)

8. Will the Revision be generally accepted ?   How is it now used ?
Is it often read in churches ?

9. State three of the popular objections to it.   What omissions
should be supplied ?

10. How long did it take the King James Version to displace earlier
ones ?

11. Did American scholarship have great influence in the revision ?
How many American suggestions were adopted ?   What are some
changes not adopted by British scholars ?   How many were made in
the New Testament ?

12. What were the principles governing the revisers ?   How were
radical changes prevented ?   How many in the Greek text ?   What
Hebrew text was followed ?   What is generally admitted respecting
the revision ?   Is the English as felicitous as the old version ?

13. Upon what version was this revision based ?   By whom was
the King James Version proposed ?   By whom ordered, and when ?
How many translators were appointed ?   When was the work begun ?
By how many scholars ?   How were they divided ?   Where did each
company meet ?   How was the work divided among them ?   [See
note.]

14. What were the principles on which King James' revision was
made ?   What other versions might be used ?

15. Was it then a new translation ?   How many of them reviewed
the finished work ?   How was it issued ?   Who wrote the introduction ?

16. Why is it called "Authorized ?"   Was it ever formally and
officially sanctioned ?   Was it cordially received ?   How was it attacked ?

17. How long was it before it finally won acceptance ?   What other
versions were in use at that time ?   Why did an early proposal to revise King James' Version fail ?

18. What changes have been made in the King James Version ?
What editions of this version are mentioned ?   Mention some noted
editions.   Which was the first to contain chronological notes in the
margin ?   Upon whose chronology were they based ?   By whom were
other marginal references inserted, and when ?

19. What was done by the Committee on Versions of the American
Bible Society in 1851–56 ?   Why was the amended edition discon-
tinued ?   What is said of the English of the King James Version ?

CHAPTER II.

(Douai, Bishops', Genevan, Coverdale's, Cranmer, Taverner, Tyndale and Wycliffe Versions.)

1. Of what was the Common Version the outgrowth? Of how many centuries' labor?

2. What is meant by the Douai Version? Why was it issued? When and where was the Rheims or Douai New Testament published? When and where was the Douai Old Testament issued? The whole Bible? To whom does this work owe its origin? What was the basis of this translation? By whom was it made? On what was the Douai Version based? How has it been changed? Has it been much used? Why? Is there any connection between this and the King James Version?

3. The Bishops' Bible, why so called? By whom was it prepared When was it completed? When and by whom was it revised? what other name is it sometimes called?

4. Why was it made? Why was the Great Bible not satisfactory?

5. How long a time was spent upon the Bishops' Version? By what four rules were its translators governed? What did this Bible contain beside the text?

6. When was the last edition issued? What rule was made by Convocation concerning it? Was it popular?

7. The Genevan version, made in what era? When and by whom was this version made? Whence does it derive its name?

8. In what year was the Genevan New Testament made? Where was it translated, by whom, and when?

9. Was that New Testament version made a part of the Genevan Bible? Where was the Genevan Bible made? Mention the names of some of the translators of the Genevan Bible. Was the New Testament in this work a translation directly from the original?

10. What were some of the merits of this translation? What kind of notes were made? How was the text printed?

11. When was it first printed in Scotland? By whom revised? How is it distinguished from others? What nickname was given to it, and why? Was it popular? How long was it under Queen Mary's ban? How many editions of the Genevan Bible were printed? How long did it retain its popularity? What was done in the first editions of King James' Version to win popularity?

12. The Great Bible, why so called? When was this version issued? By whom was the translation made? Where was it printed? What difficulties were met by the translator in its printing? What is meant by Cranmer's Bible? Whitechurch's? What was its relation to Coverdale's Bible? Where may selections from the Great Bible be

found? For how many years was the Great Bible the "Authorized Version?"

13. When was Coverdale's Bible translated? Upon what was it based? What German versions is it probable that he used? What merits had this version? What other work was done by him?

14. When was Matthew's Bible issued? Who is Matthew thought to have been? What other versions does this resemble? In what respects?

15. On what was Taverner's Bible based? Of what value is his version?

16. Tyndale's New Testament Version, when issued? What aim did Tyndale keep before him? Did he fulfil this declaration? When did he die, and how? When did he leave England?

17. Which was the first translation of the New Testament from Greek into English? Where was it issued? Describe the title page.

18. What are some characteristics of its style? How is the text arranged? How does the Lord's Prayer in it differ from other versions? Did Tyndale translate only the New Testament?

19. What do we owe to Tyndale's Version? What does Froude say of his talent? What part of the Bible was printed before this?

20. When was Wycliffe's Version made? What text was the basis of the translation? How was it issued? Who assisted Wycliffe in translating the Old Testament?

21. What is meant by Purvey's Version? Why were these versions anonymous? How many copies of Purvey's Version have been preserved? What is said of the character of this early English version? What earlier metrical versions are mentioned? By whom made? In how many ways is the name of Wycliffe spelled? What is said of the cost of a Bible in 1429?

22. Mention three important Anglo-Saxon versions of portions of the Bible. By whom were they made? What translator wrote a church history?

23. What is said of the Anglo-Saxon words in the Common English Version? Give examples of the proportion of Anglo-Saxon words in the story of Joseph. The parable of the Sower. The Lord's Prayer. How does the proportion of Anglo-Saxon of the Bible compare with that in Milton?

24. When was the first complete English Bible made? From what text? When was the New Testament in English first translated from the Greek? When was the first English Bible printed? When was the English New Testament first divided into verses? When was the English Bible so divided? State comparative cost of early English Bibles.

CHAPTER III.

MODERN VERSIONS OF THE BIBLE OTHER THAN ENGLISH, pp. 36–42.

1. Of what other versions of the Bible should English readers have some knowledge? Who chiefly made the German Version of the Bible?

2. What earlier versions of the Bible in German are noticed? What are the two theories with regard to the earlier translations? In what form was this version issued? What objections were made to the translation of religious works into German?

3. When and where was Luther's version made? Describe its title, form and illustrations. Who assisted Luther in the work?

4. How was Luther's Bible received? What did it do for the German language?

5. What original text of the New Testament did Luther use? From what was his Old Testament translated? What does Heine say of Luther?

6. What is meant by the *Probebibel?* When was it published? Mention some of the scholars connected with it. How was it received?

7. What effect did Luther's version have upon the Roman Catholics? Mention the chief Catholic versions. How do they compare with Luther's translation? Which one is now used?

8. When was the first complete translation of the Bible into *Dutch* made? By whom was it made? What did its printer suffer for his work? By whom was the next version made? On what were these versions based?

9. How long was it before another was made? How delayed? When finally begun? How long was it carried on? What name was given to this new version? What is its character?

10. Why was a new revision ordered in 1854? When completed? How received?

11. When and by whom was the first French version made? When was the first French Protestant version made? Where and by whom was it made? Mention some other French versions.

12. Describe the version by Louis Segond. Where was it printed? How many copies of the first edition?

13. What Italian versions were made before the Reformation? Whose version was prohibited by the Roman Church?

14. When and where did the first Italian Protestant version appear? In what dialect? Which versions are circulated by the Bible Society?

15. Which is the earliest of Spanish versions? Where was Regno's Version published? By whom revised? When? Describe the version published at Madrid in 1794. Which versions are now published?

16. Give the history of the Danish Bible.

17. When and by whom was the Bible translated into Swedish?

18. Into how many other languages has it been translated? Mention some of the important languages.
19. Who made the modern Arabic version? What is said of its merits?

CHAPTER IV.

ANCIENT VERSIONS OF THE BIBLE, pp. 43–51.

1. Of what value are ancient translations of the Bible to us?
2. Whence was the gospel introduced into Armenia? What was the basis of the translations of the Bible into Armenian? When did the Armenians have a written language? What version did they first use? From what manuscript does the first Armenian version seem to have been translated? By whom and where was the next translation made? What virtue does this translation possess?
3. Who translated the Bible into Gothic? What is meant by the "Western order" of the Gospels? What books are missing from this version?
4. The Coptic or Egyptian versions, in how many dialects? What versions of the Bible exist in Egypt? To what century does the first belong? How many and what manuscripts of this dialect exist? What are the advantages of this translation? What does the second version lack? How do these Coptic versions differ from ours? [See note.] What part of the Bible still exists in the Bashmuric dialect? Where is this version chiefly useful?
5. When was the Ethiopic version first made? What has now displaced it?
6. The Syriac versions: to what family of languages belong? What are the characteristics of the Syriac language?
7. Name the four Syriac versions. What is the meaning of Peshito? Which is the earliest of the four versions? Is it complete? Where and when was it found? How old is the third? Where is the best manuscript of this version? What is the date of the fourth version? Describe it.
8. In what groups may the Latin versions be classed? How old is the first of these groups? What is the basis of this translation?
9. What three types of the text are indicated? How many manuscripts are in existence?
10. Who undertook the revision of these texts, known as the Vulgate? Into what did his work develope? How long did he work and where? What are the names of the two Psalters Jerome made? How was the whole Bible finally made up? How received?
11. What is meant by the Sixtine text? Its history? The Clementine text? What is the standard text in the Roman Church?
12. When and by whom was the Septuagint version made? Why

is it called Septuagint? In what language is it? Why is this translation very important? How was it regarded by the Jews? By New Testament writers? What version did Jesus often quote? Describe Origen's Hexapla. Who were Aquila, Theodotion and Symmachus?

13. What is meant by the Targums? How many are now in existence? What are they? How have they been preserved? Of what value are they in reading the Old Testament?

CHAPTER V.

ANCIENT MANUSCRIPTS OF THE BIBLE, pp. 52–61.

1. Upon what are the oldest existing copies of the New Testament written? Of what is the parchment of the Sinaitic manuscript made? For what is the Vatican manuscript admired? Upon what were other early copies of the New Testament written? Why have many perished? What do the oldest manuscripts contain beside the New Testament?

2. How are ancient manuscripts of the New Testament classified? What three divisions were made by their contents? What three by their supposed age? How divided by the style of their writing? State a more recent division.

3. How many *uncial* MSS. are now known? Why are they called *uncial?* How many *cursives* are known? Why so called?

4. How was the text written in the early MSS.? What marks of division were found? Into how many sections was Matthew divided? Mark? Luke? John? What is said of Acts and the Epistles?

5. What is meant by *titloi?* Why not given to the first section in each book?

6. What is meant by the Ammonian or Eusebian sections? How many of these sections were there in each Gospel? How did Eusebius classify them?

7. To whom do we owe the chapter divisions in our modern Bibles? To whom the verse divisions?

8. Name the uncial manuscripts mentioned here. When, where and by whom was the Sinaitic manuscript found? Describe it. What is the Codex Augustanus? Where may printed copies of the Sinaitic manuscript be seen? What is Tischendorf's conjecture about it?

9. Of what age is the Vatican MS.? Describe it. What part of the Bible does it contain? How is it written? What is supposed to be its origin? How long has it been known to modern scholars? Whose is the last edition of this text? What is meant by the Vatican manuscript B. No. 2066?

10. Where is the Alexandrian manuscript? How long has it been there? Describe it. When and where is it probable that it was written? What does it contain beside the New Testament?

11. Which uncial MS. is in Paris ?   What is meant by a palimpsest ? How long has that been known ?   What parts of the Bible are missing from it ?   To what century does it belong ?

12. What does the Greco-Latin manuscript of Beza contain ?   Describe it.   Where is it ?   How long has it been there ?   By whom was it placed there ?

13. What is said of new MSS. ?   What new one is mentioned ? Where was it found ?

14. Why are some MSS. called *cursives ?*   To what centuries do they belong ?   How many are there ?   How classed ?

15. What is the probable date of the oldest Hebrew MS. ?   What was the rule of the old Talmudists regarding faulty or imperfect manuscripts ?   How many have been found ?

16. What are the two classes of Hebrew MSS. ?   What rules governed the copying of MSS. for synagogue use ?   What for private use ?   What do we owe to this care ?

17. How was the ancient Hebrew formerly supposed to have been written ?   How was the true form discovered ?

18. What is the Massorah ?   To what do the notes of the Massorites refer ?   How did they make corrections ?   Did they correct the text itself ?

CHAPTER VI.

THE NEW TESTAMENT: HOW AND WHEN ONE BOOK, pp. 62–70.

1. What is said of the New Testament as a book ?   How were the books made up ?   Was there any single decree selecting the books in it ?

2. How was the collection made ?   When was the line between "sacred " and " apochryphal " books first sharply drawn ?   What caused the drawing of this line ?

3. Were all books accepted with equal readiness ?   How were some books finally admitted ?   What books were so tested in the Eastern church ?   What book was questioned in the Western church ? When was the New Testament finally " closed " ?

4. How long was it allowed to remain closed ?   Who revived the discussion and on what grounds ?   What has been the general belief among Protestants in all times ?   What tests are applied to a book to decide its right to be considered one of the sacred books ?   What did Luther and Calvin say with regard to the decree of a council as a test of the sacred books ?   What creeds substantially agree in the tests ?

5. Are modern scholars disposed to accept without examination the decision of former generations ?   Are they inclined to insist upon the apostolic authorship of what they examine ?

6. What is the nature of the declarations of Councils and the Fathers

concerning the books? What tests did early Christians apply? Which book caused the Western church to hesitate? Why did they hesitate? When was it finally accepted? Whose studies lead to its acceptance? How did the Western church regard other writings than those now in the New Testament?

7. How many books were early admitted by the Eastern church? What were they called? What were the others called? How many were there? When did Eusebius write a history of the church? What does he say of the accepted books? Which books does he mention as questioned? Which were questioned by Origen?

8. What light is thrown on this research by the Fathers of the first four centuries? What adds to the value of their testimony? What list is given by Augustine? By Athanasius, Jerome and Eusebius? How are citations made by these writers? What writers are included in this reference?

9. Why were not books of the New Testament written sooner? Which two are considered the first? What allusions were made by Papias of Hierapolis? In what books is Luke's influence traceable? When were most of the New Testament books written? What made written instructions necessary? Were there heresies in the early church? By what name is the New Testament called by second century writers? How early were the twenty unquestioned books collected as Scriptures?

10. Why were the early Christians so careful in their selection? Is it improbable that the Gospels and Acts were first combined, the others being separate? What evidence is added by the circumstances under which the selections were made? What declaration concerning them was made by the Council of Carthage? Over what proportion was there any hesitation?

11. What advantage is there in this gradual sifting of the writings? What promise of Christ was fulfilled?

CHAPTER VII.

WRITERS AND COMPOSITION OF THE NEW TESTAMENT BOOKS, pp. 71–80.

1. How early were the books of the New Testament extant? How long was it before they were universally accepted? How many persons were engaged in writing the New Testament books? Were they similar in any respect to one another? What were some of Paul's characteristics? Luke's? Matthew's? John's?

2. Which were the earliest books written? Between what years may they be placed? What are the probable dates of the Synoptic Gospels and the Acts? Of the Pastoral Epistles of Paul? Of the Epistle to the Hebrews? Of the General Epistles of James, Peter and

Jude? To what period do the writings of John belong? Which the earliest? Next? Last?

3. The names of how many New Testament writers are certainly known? How many of these have been positively identified? Why is there doubt concerning the others? How are the authors of eighteen of the books known? How can the authors of the other books be found out?

4. How is it known that Matthew wrote the book called by his name? By what other name was he probably called? What does Papias say about it? What does Irenæus add to this statement?

5. What is the explanation of the fact that the Greek Gospel of Matthew reads like an original? Is there any parallel to this?

6. Who is recognized as the author of the second Gospel? With whom is he identified? With whom does Papias declare him to have been associated? What does Irenæus say of him?

7. How is it proved that the third Gospel and the Acts were from the same pen? What was the profession of their author, and how was he associated with Paul?

8. Which book was for years the chief object of attack by critics? How has the authenticity of John's Gospel been established? What objections have been made to its authorship? How can they be met? What illustration of a modern book is given? What are some characteristics that its author must have possessed, which belong only to John?

9. How many Epistles are ascribed to Paul, and on what ground? Has this evidence ever been questioned?

10. Who wrote the Epistle to the Hebrews? What was the belief in the early Eastern Church?

11. Was the Epistle of James written by John's brother? How many men bearing that name are mentioned in the Bible?

12. Is there any doubt regarding the authorship of the first Epistle of Peter? To whom was it addressed, and what was its aim? Why was the second Epistle finally accepted? What is the keynote of each book? What is the theme of both?

13. How was 1 John received by the early church? Why was it written and for whom? When was the authorship of the second and third Epistles established? To whom is the second Epistle addressed? To whom the third? When were all these Epistles written?

14. Was Jude an apostle? What incidental evidence is there respecting it? What apocryphal books does he cite? What other Epistle does this resemble? What and for whom was this letter written?

15. By whom was the Book of Revelation written? What is the character of the book? Why was it written? State the topic of each New Testament book.

CHAPTER VIII.

THE OLD TESTAMENT: HOW AND WHEN ONE BOOK, pp. 81–91.

1. During how many years was the Old Testament in process of formation? What period do the books cover?

2. What version of the Old Testament was in common use in the first centuries of the Christian era? What finally separated apocryphal from sacred books? When and by whom was an early list of Old Testament books made by a Christian writer? What statement is made by Josephus concerning the Jewish sacred books? How and why could the Old Testament books be counted twenty-two or twenty-four? Which two books are possibly uncertain in Josephus' list?

3. What does Strack say of this? Why is Josephus' evidence valuable? What of the triple division of the Old Testament?

4. How many books were counted by the Talmudists? What is the testimony of Philo regarding them?

5. How are these writings spoken of in the New Testament? Under what names are they referred to? How did Christ refer to portions of the Old Testament? What books were referred to under the name of Psalms?

6. From How many Old Testament books are quotations given in the New Testament? From how many books did our Lord quote directly? How many references are there to the Old Testament in the New Testament? What is said of Revelation in this regard? How was the Old Testament apparently divided in New Testament days?

7. When and by whom were these books definitely settled? Who were the dissenting minority? What were the views of the Alexandrian Jews? Why would the Sadducees reject some books? Where did the Samaritans stand?

8. What does Dillman consider the order of acceptance of the sacred books? What does Josephus imply as to the time when these books were all acknowleged?

9. What is the tradition regarding their selection and combination? Is this generally accepted?

10. What is the conclusion?

11. What causes account for the dissent of certain Jews from the strict list? What does Josephus say of the apocryphal books? What is the conclusion from all this evidence?

12. Is the order of the Old Testament books in the Hebrew Bible the same as in the English Bible? How many variations are noted in Hebrew copies? Are they important?

13. What was the Hebrew order of the Pentateuch? What books were included under the name " Earlier Prophets? " Under the name " Later Prophets? " What was meant by the Hagiographa? What earlier Hebrew arrangment is spoken of?

14. What assertions have been made as to variations from the list?

How do these affect the authority of the text ? What is meant by the *Patristic* list ? When and where was the *Roman Catholic* canon declared ? In what regard do these two lists agree with that of the *Greek Church* ? What inconsistencies are noted in the declarations of the *Greek Church* ? To what list does the *Protestant* canon conform ? What were Luther's views regarding the apocryphal books? What is the declaration of the Church of England concerning them? Of the Belgic and Westminster Confessions?

CHAPTER IX.

THE BOOKS OF THE LAW : THEIR AUTHORSHIP AND COMPOSITION, pp. 92–100.

With what event does the " Law " begin ? With what event does it close ? How was it originally written ? By whom arranged as now ?

1. What name is often given to these books ? What is its derivation ? By what names did the Hebrews call them ? Upon what is the unity of these books based ? How are they connected in the original ?

2. What differences of opinion as to the division of these books are mentioned ? How did Christ **speak** of them ? Whence are their English titles derived ? What is the meaning of each name ? What were their Hebrew titles ? What is the meaning of the word *Perashioth* ? How were these again subdivided ? . How often were the selections from the Law read ? Designate broadly each of the books by its contents.

3. By whom were these books written ? By whom is the question of authorship reopened ? To whom would these critics ascribe them ? How early was this inquiry raised ? What was Astruc's theory ? What was the " fragmentary " theory ? What is a third theory mentioned ? What general division of the Pentateuch is made by this " newer criticism ? " What differences of opinion have been expressed as to the date of the Pentateuch ?

4. Is there a definite avowal of authorship of the whole Pentateuch ? Quote verses to show that Moses was the author of at least a large part of the work. In what person is the book written ? What event is recorded in Deut. 34 ? What is the object of the writings ? What do they contain besides the fulfilment of this object ? What form would be most natural for the authentic record of the origin of the race ? Is knowledge of the writer of government annals of great importance ? Why not ? What would be expected of Moses as the great lawgiver of Israel ? What is the testimony of Hebrew writers as to his having done so ?

5. What evidences in the books themselves against their Mosaic authorship are urged ?

6. What evidences in favor of it ? Is there historic evidence of the existence of separate documents ? Do the critics agree among

themselves? Is it probable that the Hebrews had no written laws before the exile? Do these records agree with what we know of Egypt and other nations in the Mosaic era?

What must be accounted for on any theory? What is said of the civilization of Egypt in the Mosaic era? What is the evidence from language? Is the religious system copied from the Egyptian? What peculiarities of the worship indicate the wilderness life? Are there many characteristics of later speech in the language of the Pentateuch? What accounts for the differences between earlier and later portions? What is said of New Testament evidence?

CHAPTER X.

HISTORICAL (O. T.) BOOKS: AUTHORSHIP AND COMPOSITION, pp. 101–111.

How many historical books are there in the Old Testament? In what order do they come in the English Bible? Which is first and which last?

1. What is the Hebrew order? Which were called the Earlier Prophets, and why? How were the other six books placed? Which were the closing books?

2. How many years are covered by these books? What event opens and what closes the period? Into how many periods can the time be divided? What are they? Into what five periods may the time be divided? Give the portions of the text included in each period.

3. Who are mentioned by Jewish tradition as the chief writers of these books?

4. Whence does the book of *Joshua* derive its name? What do modern critics say concerning it? To whom do tradition and reverent scholars assign its authorship? When do they think it was composed? How can the clauses urged to prove a later date be accounted for? Of what importance is this book to the Bible student?

5. Whence does *Judges* take its name? How many judges were there? How long was this period? What reference is made by Paul to this period? To whom does the Talmud ascribe this book? Whence was it gathered? for what reason? What are the difficulties of the book?

6. When did Ruth live? When was the book probably written? Where is it placed in the Hebrew Bible? What is its historical value? What is the Jewish tradition concerning its writer? Are the arguments against an early date tenable?

7. How were the two books of *Samuel* originally written? How were the books of Samuel and Kings divided by the Septuagint? When was this division introduced into Hebrew Bibles? What is known of the author of 1 and 2 Samuel? Whence arises the name? Why could Samuel not have written both? Mention some national songs incorporated into the work. What is its date? State some difficulties.

8. What history do the two books of *Kings* continue? Whom does Jewish tradition name as the author of Kings? Who else has been named? Do they refer to older documents? What is their probable date? What new light has recently been thrown on the dynasties mentioned by these books? What difficulties are there?

9. Where were the *Chronicles* originally placed? What is the Hebrew title? What does the Septuagint call them? Who named them Chronicles? By whom were they probably written? Why were they written? What do they contain confirmatory of the Pentateuch? What date is assigned to them? How many sources are named in them? Mention them. What value have the numerous references to other sources?

10. Where was *Ezra* placed in the Hebrew Bible? What names are given to Ezra and Nehemiah in the Septuagint? In the Vulgate? Who was the author of Ezra? When was it written?

11. Where is *Nehemiah* in the Hebrew Bible? Who wrote it? What doubts are there as to its authorship? What peculiarities are mentioned in its language?

12. To what era does *Esther* belong? What peculiarity is noted in it? Why? When written? Who are named as the probable authors?

13. What is said of the twelve historical books?

14. Give the substance of Mr. Gladstone's remarks on the general character of the Old Testament books. With what does it deal?

CHAPTER XI.

HEBREW POETRY AND POETICAL BOOKS, pp. 112–122.

1. What is a leading characteristic of the Oriental mind? Were the Hebrew people affected by these feelings? What portion of the Old Testament is poetry? How does Hebrew poetry differ from that of other nations?

2. Why is there no epic poetry among them? What kinds of poetry were written in Hebrew? How does it compare with other poetry?

3. Are rhyme and meter found in Hebrew poetry? What attempts have been made to find them? Have they succeeded?

4. Of what does Hebrew poetry consist chiefly? Name and define the three kinds of parallelisms.

5. Are alliteration and assonance used? What kind of language is used by these writers?

6. How many poetical books are there in the Old Testament? Name them. Are these the only ones that contain poetry? Mention five of the most noted songs outside of these books.

7. Which is the earliest specimen of poetry in the Old Testament? How many songs are mentioned in the Old Testament? How many

are found in the New Testament? Mention them. Where are they found?

8. Where is the book of Psalms in the Hebrew Bible? Which books were regarded as preëminently poetical? What names have been given to the Psalms? Whence is the name *Psalms* derived?

9. How are the Psalms divided in the Hebrew? How are these divisions marked? What are the groups? To what have the topics of the Psalms been compared? How old is this division? What suggestions have been made as to the reasons for its existence? How many Psalms are quoted in the New Testament?

10. Were the titles of the Psalms made by their authors? To how many are they attached? What name is given by the Talmud to the others? How many Psalms are ascribed to David? To whom are the others assigned? How many are anonymous? To whom does the Septuagint ascribe the 127th? the 146th? the 147th? What famous ones are anonymous? What is said of the Hallel Songs?

11. How are the Psalms divided by their contents? How many *alphabetic* Psalms are there? Mention other classifications.

12. What is the Hebrew title of Proverbs? What is meant by the Hebrew word for proverbs? What is the essence of a proverb? What collections of proverbs are there beside the one in the Bible? How do they compare with Solomon's?

13. Was Solomon the only author of the Proverbs? Mention others.

14. How old is the complete collection?

15. What is the structure? Give examples. What is taught in this book?

16. From whom does the book of Job derive its name? To whom is the book ascribed? What indications are there in the book itself that it may have been written by Moses? To whom would modern critics ascribe it? and why?

17. What is its structure? What may it be called? Who are the dramatis personæ? What are the divisions of the book?

18. What is the object of the book? Its theme?

19. Is the book history?

20. What name is given to Ecclesiastes in the original? Why was it written? How is the idea brought out?

21. Who wrote it? Where would modern critics place it? How are the apparent discrepancies explained?

22. What is the Hebrew name of the Song of Solomon? What is its form?

23. Who wrote it? Upon what is the general belief as to its author based?

24. How is the structure of the book here defined?

25. Along what lines have interpretations been made?

CHAPTER XII.

PROPHECY AND PROPHETICAL BOOKS, pp. 123-133.

1. Who were the prophets? When were schools of the prophets established? Were all prophets thereafter taken from these schools?

2. Into how many periods may the work of the prophets be divided? What were these periods?

3. Have all the writings of the prophets been preserved? Over how many years did the existing prophecies extend? How many so-called "Later Prophets" are there? Which one was not put with the prophets by the Jews? In what form are these prophecies written?

4. How are these books divided as to form? How as to time?

5. What is the meaning of Isaiah? How does Isaiah rank? Who wrote the book? What evidence is there for his authorship of the book? What arguments are brought to bear against it? How may they be answered? Describe the structure of the book.

6. Where did Jeremiah live? To what class did he belong? Over how long a time did his prophecies extend? Who was his scribe? Describe the structure of the book.

7. Who wrote Lamentations? Of what does the book consist? What peculiarities of form are mentioned?

8. Who was Ezekiel? What is the meaning of his name? Where did he live? What is the style of his prophecy? What did the Jews declare concerning it? What are the methods of interpretation applied to Ezekiel?

9. How was *Daniel* classed by the Jews? What is the Bible testimony as to the author? What objections are urged to this? Whence sprang these objections? Describe its structure. In what languages is it written?

10. How are the minor prophets counted in the Hebrew Bible? How do they differ among themselves?

11. Who was Hosea? For how many years did he prophesy? What are the modes of interpretation of Hosea?

12. Describe Joel. What is its probable date? Where is Joel quoted in the New Testament?

13. Who was Amos? How does his style compare with that of Joel? When did he live? What is the tradition concerning his death?

14. What is the character of Obadiah's prophecy? Its date? Topic?

15. Where did Jonah live? What is the character of the book called by his name? What evidence leads us to believe the story of the great fish? Of whom was Jonah a type?

16. When and where did Micah live? Describe his style. What quotations are made from Micah in the New Testament?

17. Describe Nahum. Where did he live? His object in prophecy?

18. Who was Habakkuk? Describe his book. What quotation from Habakkuk is made in Romans?

19. What is the date of Zephaniah? What name has been given to it? What great hymn is based upon it?

20. When did Haggai write? What is the style of his book?

21. How does Zechariah rank among the prophets? What is the theme of the book? What is the Biblical testimony as to its author?

22. Which is the closing prophet? What is the meaning of his name? Describe the style of the book. Mention some of the prophecies contained in it. How does it close?

CHAPTER XIII.

CIRCULATION OF THE BIBLE, pp. 134-136.

1. Into how many languages and dialects was the Bible issued at the beginning of the nineteenth century? Into how many now?

2. How many copies of the Scriptures were circulated during the first half of the nineteenth century?

3. How many have been issued during the nineteenth century?

4. What is said of the annual issue of Bibles?

5. What is said of the circulation in heathen lands? How many added copies are needed to give each family of the world a Bible?

CHAPTER XIV.

CARE OF BIBLE TEXT, pp. 137-139.

1. What did the Jews note concerning their Scripture text besides the number of books?

2. What table is given in section two?

3. How did the Massoretes number the words and letters of the Hebrew text?

4. What did their minuteness lead some to do for the text of the English Bible? State the number of books, chapters and verses in the English Bible.

5. How many Greek words are there in the text of the first three Gospels? How many Greek words are used in the Pauline writings? How many by Luke?

6. What is the number of Greek words in the vocabulary of Luke's Gospel? How many in the first three Gospels?

INDEX.

Acts, 74
Alexandrian MS., 57. See MSS.
Alliteration, see Hebrew Poetry.
Amos, 130.
Ancient MSS., 52.
Ancient Versions, 43.
Anglo-American Versions, 7, 8.
Anglo-Saxon Versions, 33.
Armenian translations (see Versions), 43.
Authorship of Gospels and Acts, 73.
Authorized Version, why so called, 8.

Beza's MS., 58.
Books of the Law, 92.
   authorship of, 93, 94.
   composition of, 95.
   division of, 92.
   Mosaic authorship of, 96, 97.
   name of, 92.
Bible, Alexandrian (written), 57.
   Anglo-American, 8-18.
   Anglo-Saxon, 33.
   Armenian, 43.
   Authorized Version of, 12.
   Biblia by Chaucer, 7.
   Bishops', 20.
   Cambridge Paragraph, 17.
   chapters and verses in, 138.
   circulation of, 134.
   Coptic, 44.
   Coverdale's, 25.
   Cranmer's, 25.
   Danish, 42.
   divisions of, 54, 93, 137.
   Douai, 19.
   Dutch, 39.
   Egyptian, 44.
   English, facts about, 34.
   Ethiopic, 45.
   French, 40.
   Genevan. 21.
   German, 36.
   Gladstone upon the, 109.
   Gothic, 44.
   Great, 22, 23.
   greatest book, 7.
   Greek Septuagint, 49, 81.
   Hebrew, 50, 59, 60, 81-9, 101, 137.
   Holy, English title, 15.

Bible, Italian, 41.
   languages translated into, 134.
   Latin, 47.
   Luther's, 37.
   Matthew's, 26.
   Purvey's, 30.
   Taverner's, 26.
   Sinaitic (written), 52.
   Societies, 135.
   Spanish, 41.
   Swedish, 42.
   Syriac, 45, 46.
   Vatican (written), 56.
     Vulgate, 47.
   Whitechurch's, 25.
   Wyckliffe's, 29.

Chronicles, 105.
Colossians, 76-79.
Coptic or Egyptian Versions, 44.
Corinthians, 76, 79.
Coverdale's Bible, 25.
Cranmer's Bible, 25.
Cursive MSS., the, how written, 59.

Daniel, Book of, 127, 128.
Danish Versions, 42.
Date of N. T. Books, 71.
Deuteronomy (see Pentateuch), 95.
Douai Version, the, 19.
Dutch Versions, 39.

Eastern Church on N. T. Books, 65.
Ecclesiastes, 121.
Ephesians (see Pauline Eps.), 76.
Ephraem MS., 58.
Esther, 108.
Ethiopic Versions, 45.
Exodus (see Pentateuch), 95.
Ezekiel, 127.
Ezra, 87, 108.

Fac-Simile—
   Tyndale's New Testament,
              Frontispiece.
   King James's Version, 15.
   Great Bible, 23.
   Matt. 13 : 1-15, Tyndale, 27.
   Isaiah, Chap. 13, Tyndale, 13.

Fac-Simile—
early English MS. Bibles, 31.
Rushworth Gospels, John 13 : 2, 33.
Fourth Cent. Codex Sinaiticus, 55.
Fifth Cent. Codex Alexandrinus, 57.

Galatians (see Pauline Eps.), 76.
Gladstone, quotation from, 109.
Gothic Versions, 44.
Great Bible, 22.

Habakkuk, 131.
Haggai, 132.
Hebrew MS. (see MS.)
poetry, 112.
alliteration in, 113.
early songs in, list of, 114, 115.
forms of, 112.
Orientals' delight in, 112.
parallelisms of, 113.
rhyme and metre in, 112.
Hebrews, book of, 76.
Historical O. T. Books, 101.
authors of, 102–109.
general character, 109.
order of, in Hebrew, 101.
period covered by, 101.
Hosea, 129.

Isaiah, book of, 125.
Chap. 12, fac-simile of, 31.
Italian Versions, 41.

Jamnia, Synod of, 85.
James, Epistle of, 76.
Jeremiah, 126.
Lamentations of, 127.
Job, book of, 119, 120.
Joel, 129.
John's Epistles, 78.
John, Gospel by, 74.
Jonah, 130.
Joshua, 102.
Judges, 102, 103.
Jude, 78.

Kings, book of, 105.

Lamentations, 127.
Language of English Bibles, 34.
Latin Versions. 46.
Leviticus (see Pentateuch), 92.
Luther's Version, 37, 38, 63, 64.

Malachi, book of, 133.
Manuscripts, Ancient, 52.
Alexandrian, 57.
Cursives, the, 59.
divisions of, modern, 54.
Ephraem, 58.
Greco-Latin, 58.
Hebrew, 59.
classes of, 59.

Manuscripts, Hebrew, strict rules for
preparing, 59.
N. T., how written, 52.
how classified, 52.
new, 58.
sections in, Ammonian, or Eusebian,
54.
how numbered, 54.
Sinaitic, 52.
text, Divisions of, 53.
Titloi-titles, number of, 54.
Uncial, number of, 53, 55.
Sinaitic, how found, 55.
Vatican, beauty of, 52.
character of, 56.
Mark, 74.
Massorah, the, 60.
Massorites, care of Bible, 137, 138.
Matthew, 69, 73.
Matthew's Bible, 26.
Micah, book of, 131.

Nahum, 131.
Nehemiah, 107.
Nations, three foremost of the world, 7.
greatest book of, 7.
New MSS. of Bible, 58.
New Testament, one book, 62.
completion of, 68.
conclusions regarding, 69.
Eastern Church on, 65.
fresh examination of list, 64.
Luther on, 63.
Process of forming—Collection
of, 67.
unanimity of its acceptance, 63.
Western Church on, 64.
books, 71.
authorship of Gospels and Acts,
73.
character of writers, 71.
Date of the books, 71, 79, 80.
early catalogue of, 66.
Hebrews, 76.
James. Epistle by, 76.
John, Epistles by, 78.
Jude, 78.
names of writers known, 72.
Pauline Epistles, 76.
Peter, 2 Epistles by, 77.
Revelation, book of, 78, 79.
Table of, 79, 80.
variety of writing in, 71.
writers of, 72.
Numbers (see Pentateuch), 92.

Obadiah, 130.
Old Testament, one book. 81.
books quoted in the New, 84.
Ezra and the Great Synagogue, 87.
how formed, 86, 87.
Josephus on, 81, 86.

Old Testament, order of books, Hebrew, 88, 89.
    Septuagint, Books in, 81.
    Synod of Jamnia on, 85.
    testimony of Origen and Josephus to, 81.
    triple Division of, 82.
    variations, Supposed, in the lists, 89.
    what Philo and Talmudists say, 83.
        Christ and N. T. writers say, 83.
Pauline Epistles, 76.
Peter, Epistles by, 77.
Philippians (see above), 76.
Philemon (see above), 76.
Poetic books O. T., 113.
Prophecy and Prophetical Books, 123, 124.
    Ezekiel, 127.
    Daniel, author, &c., 127, 128.
    division, 124.
    Isaiah, author of, 125.
        structure of, 126.
    Jeremiah, character of, 126.
    Lamentations, 127.
    Minor Prophets, 129–133.
Prophets, great work of, 123.
Proverbs, 117, 118.
Psalms, 115, 116.
Purvey's Version, 30.

Revelation, book of, 78, 79.
Rhyme and Metre in Hebrew, 112.
Romans, Epistle to (see Pauline Eps.), 76.
Rushworth Gospels, fac-simile, 33.
Ruth, 103.

Samuel, book of, 104.
Septuagint (Greek O. T.), 49, 50, 81.
Sinaitic MS., 52.
Solomon's Song, 121.
Song of Songs, 121, 122.
Spanish Versions, 41.
Syriac Versions, 45, 46.
Swedish Versions, 42.

Table of N. T. books, 79, 80.
Targums, their character, 50.
Taverner's Bible, 26.
Text, Early Divisions of, 53.
Thessalonians, Eps. to (see Pauline Eps.), 76.
Timothy, Eps. to (see Pauline Eps.), 76.
Tischendorf, 56.
Titus, Eps. to (see Pauline Eps.), 76.
Tyndale's N. T. Version, 26–29.
Tyndale's N. T., fac-simile,
                Frontispiece.

Uncial MS., 53–55.

Vatican MSS., 52–56.

Versions, Ancient, 43.
    Armenian. 43.
    Coptic or Egyptian, three, 44.
        (1) Memphitic or Bahiric, 44.
        (2) Thebaic or Sahidic, 45.
        (3) Bashmuric or Eleaarchian, 45.
    Ethiopic, 45.
    Gothic, 44.
    Latin, (1) old Latin, (2) Vulgate, 46, 47.
    Septuagint, 49.
    Syriac, character of, 45.
    Vulgate, by Jerome, 47.
        Council of Trent on, 48.
        Sixtine edition, corrected, 48.
        Clementine Text, 49.
Versions, authorized, 8, 14.
    changes in, 17.
    charges against, 14.
Versions, Common, why so called, 8.
    editions, noted mistakes in, 17.
    principles of, 13.
    title page, fac-simile of, 15.
    why revise, 9.
Versions, Early English, 19.
    Anglo-Saxon, 33.
    Bishop's, 20.
    Coverdale's, 25.
    Cranmer's, 25.
    Douai, 19.
    Early English MSS. Bibles, 29.
        fac-simile, 31.
    Genevan, by English reformers, 21.
        New Testament, 21.
    Great Bible, 22.
        fac-simile of title page, 23.
    Matthew's, 26.
    Purvey's, 30.
    Tavener's, 26.
    Tyndale's New Testament, 1526, 26, 29.
        first, directly from Greek, 26.
        fac-simile of Matt. xiii. 1–15, 27.
    Wycliffe's, 1382, 29.
Versions, Modern, etc., not English, 36.
    Danish, 39.
    Dutch, 39.
        States' Bible, Excellence of, 40.
    French, 40.
    German, Earlier, by Romanists, 39.
    Italian, 41.
    Luther's, 37, 38.
    Arabic, 42.
    Spanish, 41.
    Swedish, 42.
Version, Revised, 8, 10.
Vulgate, 47, 48.

Western church on N. T., 64.
Writers of N. T., 72.
Wycliffe's Version, 1382, 29.